THE TAKE THAT FACT FILE

THE TAKE THAT FACT FILE

Rick Sky is the pop music editor of Britain's *Daily Mirror*, and has interviewed almost all of the world's top rock stars. He has contributed to dozens of publications all around the world, including *Spin*, *The Chicago Tribune* and *Max*, and is the author of *The Show Must Go On: The Life of Freddie Mercury*.

THE
TAKE THAT
fact file

RICK SKY

Illustrations by Andy Hunt

HarperCollins*Publishers*

HarperCollins*Publishers*
77–85 Fulham Palace Road,
Hammersmith, London W6 8JB

This paperback edition 1993
7   9   8

First published in Great Britain by
Grafton 1993

A catalogue record for this book is
available from the British Library

ISBN 0 00 638079 4

Set in Melior and Futura

Printed in Great Britain by
HarperCollinsManufacturing Glasgow

For Take That fans everywhere.

CONTENTS

IN THE BEGINNING

The early days of Take That

It was a week before Christmas and Gary Barlow's dad wanted to buy his ten-year-old son a really special present. BMX bikes were all the rage that year but Gary's dad also noticed how obsessed by pop the blond-haired youngster was.

Colin Barlow was in a dilemma – he wanted the present to be a surprise but he didn't want it to be the wrong kind of surprise, so in the end he decided to let Gary choose for himself. He told him he could either have a bike or a small keyboard.

Gary plumped for the keyboard and it was a decision that would one day change his life. It was the decision that sowed the seeds for what has become Britain's most successful teenage group since Duran Duran – Take That. For Gary was a natural musician and within a year, at the tender age of eleven, he was already playing the organ in a cabaret band where most of the other group members were in their fifties.

But even at that age, Gary dreamed of bigger and

better things. One of his greatest inspirations was the flamboyant pop star Adam Ant, who had launched himself from the remnants of the British punk scene as one of pop music's most adventurous creations.

Little Gary was transfixed. 'One day,' he mused to himself, 'I'd like to be a pop star. One day I'd like to be just like Adam Ant.' Though many people thought Adam Ant was a manufactured pop star, he wasn't at all. The songs he sang, including 'Prince Charming' and 'Stand and Deliver', were his own compositions. That struck home to young Gary – he didn't just want to be a pop star, he wanted to be a pop star who could sing his own songs.

'I loved Adam Ant. I loved his image,' says Gary. 'I think he was so appealing to youngsters. At school I put together a band with a couple of my mates that was a copy of Adam and the Ants. They had this fantastically hypnotic drum beat and we copied it by drumming on these huge biscuit tins while I sang Adam's songs over the top. That's what really started me off. I also loved the Beatles. I used to put their records on and just mime to them all day long.'

And just as Gary had a natural aptitude for the keyboard, he also had a remarkable talent for composing his own songs. His first complete songs were written at the age of thirteen and just a few years later they were tried out in his very own fledgling band, The Cutest Rush, the band that he formed with the second Take That member Mark Owen. Recalls Mark: 'I was looking for work as a singer and met up with Gary. I was just knocked out by what a brilliant keyboard player he was.'

He was more than brilliant – Gary was a man in a hurry who was already showing an extraordinary talent for writing songs.

'Before Take That was formed I already had about fifty songs written,' says Gary. 'Sometimes I used to set myself the task of writing and recording a song a day. But often the songs happened quicker than that, much quicker. "A Million Love Songs", for instance, was written in about five or six minutes when I was fifteen.

'I was very proud of it but not everyone shared my confidence. A few months after I had written it, I took it along to a music publisher to see what they thought of it. They rejected it. They said it had to be much better and much stronger to stand a chance of being published.

'Another publisher I took it to was even more brutal and cruel. I took along a tape which included that song, a tape that I had slaved over for months, getting it to what I thought was perfect. I am not going to say the name of the company I went to, but after the guy had listened to it, he took it out of the machine and then hurled it out of the window into the street below. Then he told me never to come back. I couldn't believe what he had done. It was so horrible. I was totally devastated.

'When I think back to those days it makes me laugh. The song that they turned down was exactly the same song that we had such a huge hit with. I didn't change a line.'

Mark Owen was only thirteen years old when he met up with Gary in Manchester's famous Strawberry Studios. Gary had been awarded some recording time in the studio when he won the BBC's annual 'Carol For Christmas' competition. Mark had an after-school job there.

Much of their free time was spent up in Gary's bedroom, which boasted a portable four-track recording studio where Gary was writing the songs that would one day make Take That famous. Gary was working on the cabaret circuit doing cover versions of classic hit songs but teaming up with Mark was the spur he needed to kickstart his own pop career. After forming their band, The Cutest Rush, they decided they needed to find some work so, armed with a demo tape, they went along to the entertainment agency run by Nigel Martin-Smith.

A few months later two more fresh-faced teenagers, Howard Donald and Jason Orange, turned up at Martin-Smith's agency. The two had been in rival Manchester break-dance groups until they decided to join forces and form their own dance group, Street Beat. Break-dancing was the most athletic type of dancing the pop world had ever seen. Originally developed on the streets of New York, the dancers were nothing short of disco acrobats, performing somersaults, backflips and headspins in the hope of earning some money from the astounded passers-by.

Howard and Jason were ambitious and took their form of disco busking into the local clubs where they would be paid £25 a night for their fancy flips and spins. Jason's dancing already had a wide audience as he appeared regularly on Pete Waterman's late-night TV show, *The Hitman and Her*. And it was during one of the shows that Jason first met up with Martin-Smith.

'Break-dancing was something that a lot of kids did because it kept them out of trouble on the streets,' says Jason. 'It was a big craze for a couple of years around 1983 and I got really into it. I wanted to be a dancer more than anything else. I didn't really want to be in a pop group. I dreamed about dancing in front of thousands of people and really putting on a spectacular show.'

When Jason and Howard strolled into Martin-Smith's office that warm summer day they were looking for advice. They wanted some help in their dancing career and thought Nigel might be just the man to guide them. But Nigel had other ideas. He had a brainwave – he put two and two together and got a group. Howard and Jason were the perfect pair to team up with those two other youngsters, Gary and Mark, who had come to him earlier. And so Take That was conceived.

But Martin-Smith wasn't quite satisfied. He thought the foursome lacked one thing – a fifth member. And he already had an idea of who it might be. A Stoke-on-Trent lad Robbie Williams, who had high hopes of becoming an actor, had just signed up with the agency and Nigel thought he would be perfect. Robbie met the rest of the band and went along for his audition. The others took to him straight away and so Take That was complete.

The formation of Take That was a dream that Martin-Smith had long nurtured. A vision of the perfect teen group had constantly invaded his everyday business thoughts. He had set himself the strictest of standards – he wanted all the members of the group to be talented, good-looking, energetic and totally committed. With the creation of Take That he believed he had such a band.

One thing that immediately singled his group out was just how young they were – Mark and Robbie were both only sixteen, Gary was nineteen and Jason and Howard were twenty. When they signed their contract with Martin-Smith in September 1990 he insisted that some of their parents were there, too. Marjorie Barlow was impressed when Nigel advised Gary to bring along a parent. 'You hear so many things about the crookedness of the music business and about bad management, and he wanted to set everybody's mind at ease and show that everything was above board.'

A year of hope and hardship, delight and despair was to follow the signing of that contract. The first thing they did was sit down with manager Nigel Martin-Smith and talk about how they were going to take on the pop world. They talked almost daily for the first few months about the songs they were going to sing, the act they were going to perform and the image they wanted. It was a period where they did little more than practise, talk and dream. 'Really the band was nothing for those first six months,' recalls Gary. 'It was a very odd period. We had all come together because Marky and myself were looking for management, then we were hooked up with Jason and Howard and finally Robbie. We were then told to go off and see if we could write something or come up with anything. It was very off-the-cuff stuff.

'Nigel was originally interested in my writing and when we first met I thought he was going to get me a publishing deal because that's what we always spoke about. For a long time the band just didn't seem real.'

But the band most certainly was real and the first thing they needed to prove they existed was a name. The problem was solved one day when the guys saw a picture of pop superstar Madonna. 'It was a very raunchy picture of Madonna,' remembers Mark, 'above which was written the caption "Take That". We had spent weeks agonizing over a name, but this just struck all of us. We thought it was snappy and had a punch to it.

'At first we decided to call ourselves Take That and Party, but we dropped the "Party" bit when we heard about the American group The Party. We knew we had something original to offer and we wanted to make sure our name was original, too.'

They had chosen their name – next came their image. They found their first look courtesy of the fashionable shopping district on Kensington High

Street, London. It was Jason who chose it for them. 'We were on our way to Hyper Hyper when we walked past this leather shop and Jason saw this jacket with tassels hanging off it that he really wanted,' says Mark. 'So he went off and bought it. And then the whole group had to find jackets that matched it.'

Early publicity pictures of Take That show the band wearing sequinned codpieces over tight leather trousers. It was a strange mix, part wholesomeness and part danger. It was a style they would later ditch when they decided that the mean and tough leather look was too much at odds with their clean-cut image. Nick Wilson, former executive producer with *The Hitman and Her*, who gave the band one of their first breaks on the popular TV show, remembers the original look: 'The boys always wore leather jackets in the early days. But as far as I can recall, their success happened when they took all that leather gear off and started to look more like they do in real life. They blossomed when they appeared like a bunch of normal lads.

'I suspect they had some misguided image-building in the beginning.'

Today Gary won't be drawn into admitting that their fetish-style leather was a mistake: 'I don't know if it was. We're here now because of all the things that happened to us in the early days. It's hard to know what was a mistake and what was a plus. I mean, I must admit I look back now and think "oh no" about the way I looked in all that leather and the way I used to have my hair. But they were fun times for us then. We all enjoyed it and even though we didn't have any hits we were getting our name around and getting recognized, so I don't really regret anything from that time.'

The leather look was showcased at the band's very first show in the nearby Lancashire town of Huddersfield. 'There were about twenty people in the audience and a dog,' remembers Gary. 'Only about ten of them were watching but to be honest I was glad because I felt I was messing a lot of things up. We really didn't care that only a few people had bothered to see us. It was our first gig and we were just so excited about performing that it wouldn't have mattered if only the dog was watching. Besides, we didn't notice the audience, we were much too busy concentrating on the songs, the music and our dance steps. Afterwards we were on such a high.'

Twenty people and a dog might not be the stuff that pop legends are made of, but it was at least a beginning.

*

Shortly after this the band had a wonderful stroke of luck – a TV appearance. It was a great break. Some bands wait years to get a slot on a TV show and some never manage to get one at all. Yet here was a band who had only just been formed on a programme that could bring their music to millions.

That first appearance was on a music show called *Cool Cube*, a programme on the now defunct satellite channel BSB.

It was the television appearance that finally convinced Gary that the band were not a figment of somebody's imagination but real flesh and blood: 'It all changed when Nigel came along one day and said that he thought we had a chance of doing some TV and we should get something together for it. I wrote a song called "Waiting Around" and took it to the other lads. They thought it was good and devised a bit of a routine. Then we showed it to Nigel. He liked it and then sprung another surprise – he said we needed two songs because that was probably what the TV programme would ask us to do. So, I had to rush away and dash off another song, called "Girl", and the rest of the guys had to quickly get together another routine.'

Former *Cool Cube* producer Ro Newton recalls: 'Nigel contacted me and said he had this really good band for the programme and he asked me what the chance was of getting them on the show. He brought the lads in to meet me and I was very impressed – they had a great dance routine and smashing voices. They appeared on the show a few times because they were so popular and we had such a great response to them.'

The band were determined to cause a sensation on the shows. On one occasion they wore red velvet bomber jackets and excruciatingly tight black cycling shorts which didn't leave much to the imagination. 'We were a little dubious about the tight cycling shorts in the beginning,' says Ro. 'They were rather risqué.'

From the very beginning, Nigel Martin-Smith was the driving force behind the band, constantly encouraging and motivating them to always give their best shot at everything.

Ro, a former *Smash Hits* journalist, saw Nigel in action: 'Before their first TV appearance Nigel gave them a real pep talk like a coach in a dressing room before a big match. The boys appeared a bit apprehensive because it was their first show. But they never showed any signs of being cocky, they were always eager to please. At times Nigel appeared like a father towards the band as he was very protective of them. But he was also strict with them and would have a go if he thought they looked sloppy or weren't working hard enough. Sometimes I thought he was too hard on them because they did push themselves.'

After appearing on *Cool Cube* the band went on to star on *The Hitman and Her*. It was another big break for them. The show, which had fast become a must for all young dance fans, was the brainchild of pop mogul Pete Waterman. Affable, motor-mouthed Waterman hosted the show himself together with pretty TV presenter Michaela Strachan. It was fast, played the latest dance songs and was above all fun. And it was a great place to check out fresh, new talent. Gary acknowledges what an important show it was for the novice band to do: 'When we did the *Hitman*, all of a sudden everyone started getting interested in us. It was so exciting. We set up a few gigs and started doing them.'

Former producer of *The Hitman and Her* Angie Smith remembers the band very well. 'When I first met Take That I thought they looked like five good-looking boys from next door. The teenage girls loved them as they appeared so accessible, not like Prince or Michael Jackson.

'I remember when they appeared on the show they performed their debut single, "Do What U Like", which caused a real stir.'

TV appearances are important to a new band but even more so is a video. The band knew they had to get a video for their first single that would get them noticed, that would stand out from the hundreds of videos that are released every week. In the end their very first video did more than get their faces on TV – it got their bare behinds on film, too.

The video for 'Do What U Like' was shot in one day in Stockport and it revolved around jelly, dance routines and the band's naked bottoms. Co-producers Ro Newton and Angie Smith were brought in, on a tight budget, to make the video.

'When we had our first meeting with the band we went to a rehearsal room in Manchester and they showed us their dance routine,' says Angie. 'I thought they were absolutely brilliant and as far as I was concerned they had the makings of the perfect pop band. They all looked very good and they were excellent dancers.

'At first the manager wanted the video to be based around a dance routine but I thought that might be boring. As it was their first video I knew we needed to spice it up and make it outrageous to help them make a big impact.

'The original idea was to have one close-up of a bare bottom with a piece of red jelly wobbling around on it. We wanted to add some mystery by making people wonder whose bum it was. The bottom shot was the last one we did and it proved to be hilarious. All of a sudden all the guys started arguing about whose bum we were going to choose. In the end we decided the best thing to do was to audition them all to settle the argument. It was the end of the day and we were really tight for time so we just said, "OK, all of you get your trousers off." It was amazing. I have never seen five people strip off so quickly in my life before. They all laid down on their fronts and that made a very good shot. Gary was the most embarrassed – he started to blush and tried to cover up his bum with a towel – while Robbie was very keen.'

Ro Newton recalls how Howard was the most daring of all: 'He ended up shaking on all fours, revealing everything. We laughed ourselves silly but anticipated that it might be a bit of a problem.'

According to the producers, different versions of the video were edited, including one suitable for young fans and an X-rated version for adults. 'I was bright red and embarrassed,' says Gary. 'But the others didn't seem to have any inhibitions. They couldn't wait to get their gear off. As we showed our bums everyone from the models to the video crew just stood around looking.'

After the video shoot was over a very pleased Nigel invited everyone out for a meal at Bredbury Hall in Stockport. 'That night Gary got up and played piano in the restaurant,' remembers Angie. 'I could not believe it, he was brilliant. He played a lot of ballads, including songs by Barry Manilow and Lionel Richie – the sort of thing that would move your mother to tears. Everyone in the restaurant, from the other guests to the waiters, thought he was great. I realized there and then what a talented musician and singer he was.'

The jelly video was premiered on *The Hitman and Her* on 12 July 1991, to tie in with the release of the single.

Robbie's sister Sally remembers how the Williams family reacted when they saw the video. 'We were all shocked at first because it was very cheeky!' she admitted.

Despite the fun video and the great hopes, their first single didn't exactly take Britain by storm. It was left languishing at number 82 in the charts and the five fresh-faced guys who hoped to be the pop phenomenon of the nineties were devastated and dejected.

MAKE OR BREAK

The ups and downs of the first year

Good songs and a good stage show are not enough to get a band to the top. A group who really want to make it have to surround themselves with the right people – a dynamic manager, sympathetic record bosses and a whizz-kid record plugger to get their songs played on the radio and TV.

Another key person in the team is the press officer. Their job is a crucial one: to make sure the band get their names, faces and stories in the papers and magazines across the nation.

Take That's first press officer was Carolyn Norman. She was so convinced the band would be famous that she gave up her job to represent them!

'The band's manager, Nigel, kept saying he had this great band he wanted me to see,' recalls Carolyn. 'He thought I would be just right to work for them. When I saw them I was completely knocked out – I thought they were fantastic and had an amazing stage presence. Girls were going wild for them and it was clear to me they were going to be absolutely massive.' So she ditched in her job at Atlantic Radio to take up the challenge of turning this unknown band into the most famous teen sensation of the nineties.

Carolyn started working for Take That in April 1991, about three months before the release of the band's first single, 'Do What U Like', and through a powerful media campaign she helped transform them into teen stars.

In the early days she travelled with the band wherever they went – to clubs, radio promotions, TV appearances and even shopping centre signings. It was a non-stop gruelling schedule designed to make Take That famous – and it worked. Take That were splashed across the pages of all the teen magazines and became a name on teenage lips before they had even had a hit. 'After a while it was just wild,' says Carolyn. 'I had never seen anything like it. Wherever they went the kids would try and kiss them and grab them and hang on to their car – it was really crazy.

'The schedule was an absolute nightmare as they worked virtually every single day and night. They started off on a club tour and did as many as three or four shows a night.'

In the early days the five members of the band crammed into Gary's car or borrowed Nigel's XR3i to get to venues. Later they took to the road in hired yellow vans, after Gary sold his car to buy a new keyboard.

Carolyn remembers the exhausting drives: 'The band couldn't afford to stay in plush hotels in those days. Instead, they would drive all the way to shows and then drive all the way back in the early hours of the morning. But the boys didn't mind. To pass the time they would have a good old singsong on those long and tiring journeys.'

Gary would often entertain the band if there was a piano around and they could always rely on Robbie to keep their spirits up and have them in stitches with his non-stop barrage of jokes and pranks. But as the band pursued fame they waved goodbye to long-term girlfriends and any normal family life. 'They worked so hard I don't think they had any time for girlfriends,' remembers Carolyn. 'I think maybe Jason and Gary had girlfriends in the beginning and I think Howard had just split up from someone. But they all realized that if they were going to make a go of it with the band they had to sacrifice having relationships.'

Song-writer Gary rarely had a moment to himself. When he wasn't performing, he was composing songs for the band's debut album. 'When the others had time off, Gary would be working, he would sit and write songs. He has this kind of quietness that allows him to just sit down and compose a love song.'

Although there was no evidence of personality clashes or rows, the band did occasionally needle Robbie. 'They picked on Robbie at one gig, saying that he hadn't got a dance step right,' remembers Carolyn, 'even though he was working really hard. But if they did have big arguments, they certainly hid it very well. I never witnessed any.'

Gradually all the hard work began to pay off and Take That started to appear in the teen magazines and even the national press. In June 1991 they featured in *My Guy*, *Jackie* and *No 1*, and in July *Smash Hits* followed suit. In August they clinched their first ever front page, in *No 1*, and *Just Seventeen* mentioned them on the cover and devoted five pages to the band inside. The Take That blitz was beginning.

'I went round to all the teen magazines and showed them pictures of the band and a video,' says Carolyn. 'It was at a difficult time because people weren't really that interested in new bands. But when they saw what they had to offer they really went for them. In the beginning we bullied and cajoled people to get them to see the band but once they did they were full of support.'

Despite the big response from the teen magazines other music biz bigwigs were not so forthcoming. They were not prepared to publicize the band until they had proof of their musical abilities – not least a Top Forty hit. Sometimes Carolyn's efforts were cruelly frustrated: 'The Radio 1 Road Show refused to feature Take That in June 1991 because they said they weren't famous enough. Nor did they support the first single, "Do What U Like". It was a blow but there was nothing we could do about it. And when we first approached the makers of the TV show *Ghost Train* they didn't think they had got what it took to appear on the show.'

At the same time as the fivesome were blitzing the media, they were constantly on the road making radio appearances and doing shows on their club tour. But things didn't always go according to plan. 'One gig we did at the very beginning for Signal Radio was quite a disaster as it had been raining and the group kept slipping and sliding all over the stage,' remembers Carolyn. 'It was very comical but not exactly the kind of impression we wanted to create. I had told the radio station that the band was going to be massive, but it was extremely hard to believe looking at the way they performed.

'About a year later Signal put them on in a local nightclub in the Stoke area and said they could have sold it out ten times over. They admitted then that I'd been right to predict the band would be massive.'

Take That also had problems at a show for Beacon Radio in Wolverhampton when the sound system broke down. 'At the time we didn't have the single cut for "Do What U Like" so we had to take a cassette to the show,' says Carolyn. 'Unfortunately they didn't have any facilities for playing the tape. There was a real panic. In the end they managed to rig up a ghetto blaster to the equipment and play the tape through that. But the music didn't come over well at all. The audience just didn't know what was going on.'

But it wasn't long before the band got their act together and began to attract crowds of wild fans who would do anything to be near them. Carolyn remembers one occasion vividly: 'At Hollywoods nightclub the girls were so desperate to see the band they smashed this plate glass window to get in. That was the kind of madness, frenzy and mayhem there was in the early days. After the show the boys had to race off in their van and they were followed by a mob of girls, who were in turn chased by parents who were trying to catch up with them. It was bizarre.'

On one occasion a crazed fan went too far when she ripped off Mark's favourite necklace. 'Mark had a lovely crucifix on a leather string which he bought to go with all the leather gear the band were wearing at that stage. He didn't mind giving away the bandanas that he always wore, but he got upset when a fan stole his necklace as it meant a lot to him.'

In general Take That had excellent relations with their fans, as they proved to two competition winners who, thanks to *Jackie* magazine, won the chance to meet the boys – even though their parents were not entirely happy about it. 'When the band turned up in their van to pick up one girl winner, her father freaked,' admits Carolyn. 'He saw these five gorgeous-looking lads and he didn't want his daughter to go with them. In the end we managed to convince him and she went with the band to Alton Towers and had a brilliant time.'

Despite their growing legions of fans and the media coverage surrounding them, they had serious worries about whether they would ever become a chart force to be reckoned with.

After their first single bombed they had a crisis

of confidence. 'In the beginning all the record companies turned us down,' remembers Nigel. 'It was a rotten feeling and very depressing but I wouldn't be beaten. I knew the band had talent and that talent would eventually get them through.'

He was right. Interest was growing in the band as record companies became aware of just how big Take That's fan following was. Nick Raymond, head of A&R at RCA Records, decided to find out for himself what all the fuss was about. 'There was such a big buzz about them, especially from the teen magazines, that I went along to see them perform. The first show I went to was in Slough and I was really impressed by how they got the crowd on their side and won them over with their sheer enthusiasm.'

He was so impressed that he offered the band a record contract, and in September 1991 the deal was clinched. Nigel and the band were ecstatic, but there was no time to celebrate – there was work to be done.

Equipped with a record deal and a new image – they ditched the leather in favour of string vests – Take That set off on a three-week regional tour of under-eighteen clubs to promote 'Promises', their second single. Their mode of transport to and from the shows reflected their new status as a top priority for their record company. Gone were the battered cars and vans, and in their place was a flashy Renault Espace financed by the record company. They even began to taste the delights of staying in hotels, rather than driving home through the night after each gig.

When 'Promises' was released in November 1991 the band waited in suspense to see how it would do. 'The Sunday evening "Promises" made the chart we were all gathered round a radio in a hotel room, sprawled around on chairs resting our aching limbs,' remembers Jason. 'When they announced it was number 38 we all jumped on to each other and then leaped on to the bed, which we broke. Nigel cracked open the champagne, we celebrated and then went off to do a show a little bit tipsy.'

November was a bumper month for media coverage and you could hardly turn on the TV without seeing their faces on shows as diverse as *Wogan, Going Live, O-zone, Motormouth* and *Pebble Mill*. But the band's initial excitement at their Top Forty chart entry was short-lived as the single failed to move beyond number 38. Determined to do better, they put all their energies into working on their debut album over Christmas and the New Year.

But the road to fame and success was destined

to be a rocky one for Take That. The real crisis point came in January when their third single 'Once You've Tasted Love' only reached a lowly number 47 in the charts. When the band heard the news their emotions got the better of them. That night in the small and depressing bed and breakfast hotel where they were staying, they broke down and cried. Tears of frustration, tears of anger, tears of disappointment. Worse was to come the next day when RCA told them that plans to release their first album had now been put on ice.

The band's critics who had given the group a rough ride, dismissing them as brainless puppets, put the boot in further and rumours raced round the pop world that the band were set to split up. It wasn't too far removed from the truth – for Take That the future suddenly looked bleak.

'I was very worried,' admits Robbie. 'I was convinced I'd have to forget about a pop career and go back to college. It looked as if we were going nowhere.'

'We talked very seriously about splitting up around that time,' says Gary. 'If the next record had been a flop we wouldn't have been able to carry on. Though we had thousands of loyal fans, somehow we just couldn't seem to break through. We were having trouble getting our records played on the radio and whatever we tried to do to get a big hit just didn't seem to work. But we decided not to be beaten. We knew we had something to offer. We weren't going to give up.'

The band had a crisis meeting to discuss the future and lots of problems were thrashed out. They knew they had to do something extraordinary if they were to salvage their dreams of pop stardom. Eventually they hit upon the idea of a mammoth tour of schools and youth clubs – if the fans wouldn't come to the music, then the music would come to the fans. It would mean three months of doing five or six shows a day, an incredible workload, but it was the tour that was to change their fortunes for ever.

The tour was put together in conjunction with the Family Planning Association, and was dubbed the Safe Sex tour. The Association saw it as an ideal opportunity to get across the importance of safe sex, contraception and the danger of unwanted pregnancy to thousands of school-children. To the band, it was a great way to meet their fans and do something really worthwhile at the same time.

'It was great fun,' recalls Gary. 'We loaded up the car with two speakers, an amplifier, a tape deck and a microphone and went around to all the various schools that were keen for us to perform.'

They sang their songs, gave out FPA leaflets and had mini discussions with the kids about sex, AIDS, drugs, smoking – anything they wanted to talk about. 'I felt really good when the kids were asking our opinions and advice about these kinds of things,' Gary says. 'I felt as if we were helping. The kids really opened up to us and I loved that.'

The tour was a fantastic success. 'The kids were very interested in talking,' says Jason, 'and a lot of teachers came up to us afterwards and thanked us for what we had done. I think we were on their wavelength and that was why we could communicate so well.'

'Take That were very courageous to associate themselves with the Safe Sex campaign,' says Ann Furedi, former press officer with the FPA. 'I was very struck by the incredibly responsible attitude they have towards sex. They helped us a great deal by putting our message across to an audience we couldn't normally reach.'

In the meantime, the band had taken the decision to release a cover version of the Tavares classic 'It Only Takes a Minute' as their third single. Chart success was just around the corner . . .

ON THE ROAD

Take That conquer Britain

Take That were given the royal seal of approval by Princess Margaret in May 1992 when she told the band she loved their raunchy dance routines. Her Royal Highness became one of Take That's most famous fans after they attracted her attention at the Children's Royal Variety Performance which was held at London's Dominion Theatre.

When it was the band's turn to meet their first member of the Royal Family face to face they were all on their best behaviour. 'When we met the Princess she told us how much she loved our dancing and our songs,' said Jason. 'In fact she stayed talking to us for quite a while and she even cracked some jokes.'

Robbie was thrilled to meet Her Highness, who told him she loved the band's dance routines. 'She said that she was very impressed with our performance,' he reported, while Gary recalled Princess Margaret's comment on their fans in the audience: 'She said she heard all of our fans screaming for us.'

After the band's royal encounter all their months of hard slog were eventually rewarded in June when 'It Only Takes a Minute' shot into the charts at number 16 and eventually soared to number 7. It was an old soul hit from the mid seventies from American group Tavares but Take That gave it a new treatment.

'We all thought recording an oldie might do it for us,' recalls Jason. 'So we got together with stacks of records, playing our way through them, looking for the right song, and when we heard the Tavares song we knew that was exactly the right song for us.'

Take That were euphoric when they heard that the record had gone in at number 16, making it the highest chart entry since the beginning of their pop career. But even at the height of their ecstasy the band did not forget those loyal fans who had put the record in the chart. 'As soon as we heard the chart we ran out to see the fans,' says Mark. 'They were rushing around the streets outside screaming their heads off. I think they were even more excited than we were! My family were over the moon, too, but I couldn't speak to them for over an hour because my phone was busy all that time with people ringing in to my home to congratulate me.'

Robbie was as thrilled as all the others when he heard the single's chart position. 'It was absolutely brilliant. We were over the moon, gobsmacked.'

A week after the hit single entered the charts the band were back on the promotional treadmill, appearing on a Radio 1 Road Show live from Alton Towers. Gary's mum was full of emotion as she listened to the screaming fans on the radio from her family home in Cheshire. 'Hearing those girls scream and scream, I realized that all that Gary had been working for and dreamed about all those years had been achieved. There were tears in my eyes.'

Take That had another hit single in August with 'I Found Heaven' which reached number 15 in the charts. Now – finally – the band's debut album could be released. When *Take That And Party* came out, I wrote in the *Daily Mirror*, 'It hasn't been easy for Take That to break into the big time. Now their debut album will change all that.' It wasn't a hard prediction to make. Take That were now a force to be reckoned with and the album's soaraway sales proved that. It reached number 2 in the charts, proving that Take That were here to stay.

After the album was released the band set off on their biggest yet in-store signing tour and were besieged by fans everywhere they went; 3,000 fans turned up in London, 2,000 in Glasgow and York and an incredible 5,000 in their hometown Manchester. The situation became so dangerous at the Manchester HMV store that the group had to be smuggled out disguised as policemen to stop them being mauled and hurt by the crush of hysterical fans. Four fans were rushed to hospital suffering from breathing problems, after being crushed in the crowd. In the end HMV pulled the plug on signings in Leicester, Nottingham, Reading and Croydon over fears about the safety of fans.

The band were devastated when they were forced to cancel the rest of the signings. 'Once again it's the kids who suffer,' said Gary. And he asked me to make it clear that cancelling the record store sessions was nothing to do with the band but was forced on them by the fears of the police and store bosses.

After HMV made the decision to cancel the remaining signing sessions, manager Nigel Martin-Smith fumed: 'The boys are really gutted for those fans who planned to see them and now will be bitterly disappointed. They hate letting their fans down. We think it would have been fairer to the girls to take out more security at the other venues instead of cancelling.

'The band are very concerned for fans' safety and the last thing they want is a massive crush. As soon as they saw that the situation was getting out of control they planned their escape.'

A spokesman for HMV said: 'We felt there was a high risk that someone was going to get badly hurt so we decided to cancel the rest of their appearances at our stores.'

The panic and crush at the Manchester HMV store was just one of many scenes of Take That fan mania which followed them wherever they went. When they took to the stage at Spirals nightclub in Yate near Bristol ecstatic girls mobbed them and screamed and stamped until the band gave them an encore. After the show fans fought desperately to catch a glimpse of the boys as they followed them in convoys along motorways to their next venue.

In September Take That appealed to a wider audience with the release of a ballad, 'A Million Love Songs'. Ballads are a traditional way of attracting all kinds of listeners, especially older ones, and Take That wanted to show that they could appeal to everyone, not just the teenage fans.

It was time to tour.

*

Take That conquered Britain one cold November day in Newcastle. November 2 1992 was the date that their first major British tour started. It was also the day that transformed them into a household name.

When I went up to report on the first date of the tour for my column in the *Daily Mirror*, I went with all the enthusiasm of a pop critic about to be subjected to the latest 'teen' sensation.

I had seen teen bands come and go and, quite frankly, most of them had left me cold. Duran Duran, Wham, Jason Donovan, Bros and New Kids on the Block weren't exactly the most played records in my collection. So this afternoon when I caught the train up to Newcastle with *Mirror* photographer Chris Grieve, though not blindly prejudiced, I wasn't expecting any great shakes.

I was in for a wild surprise because that night the band were hot stuff. Though the show was carefully rehearsed and planned, I was very impressed by the group's slick singing, dancing and music.

In Wednesday's *Daily Mirror* I devoted a whole page to them.

They may seem like an overnight success, but they are not. Take That have been slaving on songs and

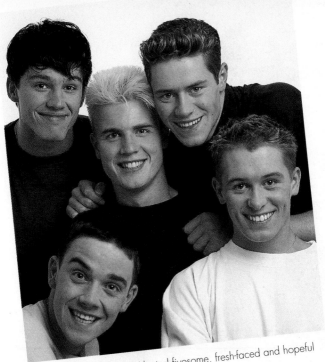

▲ An early picture of the talented fivesome, fresh-faced and hopeful

▼ Spot the extrovert!

▲ The band model their original leather look ▼

▲ 'How does this go on?' asks a puzzled Jason. 'I haven't a clue,' says Howard

▲ Mark begs for mercy as the band shoot the video for
'Do What U Like', while Howard and Jason bend over
backwards to please ▼

▲ Take That in a party mood and getting out and about ▼

▲ A steamy shot, their bodies glistening with sweat and – red jelly?

▼ Robbie seems to have bitten off more than he can chew

▶ Could Gary be on the phone to his hairdresser?

◀ A pre-beard Jason smiles sweetly for the camera

▲ Mark – and *that* grin

▲ Howard, break-dancer extraordinaire, gives us his enigmatic look

dance steps for the last three years. Now all the dreams have finally come true. On Monday night they launched their sell-out British tour in New-castle – a tour that will establish them as Britain's latest teen idols.

The group, who are currently enjoying their biggest hit, socked it to all the carping critics who said they would never make it big when they kicked off their British Tour at Newcastle City Hall. The pop world's latest teen sensation sent over 2,000 girl fans into spasms of ecstasy during their one-and-a-half hour session.

The last time a British band caused such hysteria was during the height of Brosmania. As teen idols go, they have a lot to offer. They have better songs than Bros, they are better looking than New Kids on the Block and they have more dynamism than Jason Donovan and Chesney Hawkes.

But what really sets them above their rivals is their sheer energy and enthusiasm.

They could also give Michael Jackson a run for his money when it comes to dancing. Some of their routines – which include back flips, somersaults and break-dancing – were breath-taking. They are also capable of writing good songs, as the current ballad smash 'A Million Love Songs' testifies.

They give teenage fans exactly what they want – there are plenty of suggestive hip thrusts and grinds and lots of bare flesh and rippling muscles. Before the band appeared on stage they teased the already frenzied crowd with a few bars of 'It Only Takes a Minute' and then they materialized for real, kicking off with 'Do What U Like'. By the time they finished with 'Take That and Party', not only were the group drained, physically and emotionally, but so were their audience.

After the show finished I met up with the band in the bar of the hotel where we were all staying. They were as fun and as down-to-earth as ever, incredibly polite and well-mannered. After a big show a lot of bands get delusions of grandeur – nothing excites the ego so much as an adoring audience – but if Take That's egos were big that night they certainly didn't show it.

As we talked I realized just how long they had planned and dreamed about this night. All of them had been involved in music and dancing since their early teens and all of them were perfectionists when it came to their craft. But the biggest knock-out blow came when Gary revealed that he had written 'A Million Love Songs' when he was just fifteen, and he had composed dozens of other songs at that age too. I was impressed – 'A Million Love Songs' is in the same league as George

Michael's 'Careless Whisper', a pop ballad classic. Contrary to some of the publicity, I realized that the songs and stagecraft were basically all their own work. Yes, there was plenty of hype and hullabaloo surrounding them, but underneath was a bedrock of talent.

Gary revealed that the band's current smash had taken just five minutes for him to write. 'I forgot all about the song until a year later when we signed our first record contract. Most of my songs take about fifteen minutes to finish completely. I play them to my mum and gran. If they like them – we use them.'

The band fought a long hard battle to get 'A Million Love Songs' released. 'We had made our name as a dance band,' said Gary, 'and a lot of people thought that if we released "A Million Love Songs" it would be the kiss of death. But we had faith in the song and wanted it out. There were a lot of rows but in the end we got our way. And we were proved right. That song has changed our careers.'

The weeks leading up to the band's first major British tour were fraught with tension, nerves and problems. At one time Jason thought he might have to pull out of the tour after a nasty accident during rehearsals. Jason, who sported his Mohican hairstyle during the tour, pulled a hamstring during one of the group's frenzied dance routines.

'I was in absolute agony,' said Jason. 'I was rushed to see a doctor who told me to stop dancing. He said that if I carried on I could risk permanent injury. I just didn't know what to do. It was two weeks before the first show of the biggest tour we had ever embarked on and I didn't want to let them down, but at the same time I didn't want to risk damaging myself badly.

'I had to stop dancing and the doctor gave me some injections – luckily just a few days before the show everything got better and I was given the all clear.

'The day before the Newcastle show we did three rehearsals – including two full dress rehearsals. We were all so knackered – especially me. I thought my body was going to fall apart. Before the show I was actually aching all over, but once you're out there on stage in front of a screaming crowd, the adrenalin starts pumping and you forget all your aches and pains. My hamstring didn't bother me one bit. The crowd is the best doctor there is.'

As the minutes ticked away before the curtain came up on that first show, emotions got to fever pitch. Howard broke down in tears just seconds before they took the stage, as they waited to step out in front of over 2,000 adoring fans.

'I just couldn't control myself,' he admitted. 'It was just such an emotional moment. Suddenly everything we had worked for and dreamed of was about to happen. I'm not soft, but you would have to be made out of stone not to have felt the power of that moment.'

Robbie was in the wars too: 'I had to go and see a throat specialist just before the tour started. My throat was giving me so much pain. One day it was so bad, I couldn't get to sleep at all.'

The screams that night were so loud that the next day over breakfast Gary woke up with his ears still hurting. 'I have never heard anything so loud in all my life,' he said. 'The crowd was just excellent.'

The experience of Newcastle was to be repeated over and over again on that sell-out tour as the band converted thousands of new fans to the Take That cause. Towards the end of the tour, the band came to London to play the famous Hammersmith Odeon. Afterwards they held a party at their hotel. Hundreds of Take That fans, with the kind of ingenuity that Columbo would be proud of, had found out where the band was staying and were waiting outside for them. Inside were a mass of journalists, record company workers and band friends. The Take That charm was much in evidence that night as they moved from group to group, chatting amiably away to everybody in the room.

The hard work was almost over and the boys just couldn't hide their happiness at how well everything had gone. It was obvious how much they were enjoying themselves – their smiles said it all. And it wasn't just the fans outside who were smitten by their charm. Inside, many of the women from the record company and the press – much older than the band – were bowled over by their looks and their style.

Then at 12 o'clock the band suddenly disappeared, like five Cinderellas fleeing from the ball, and the bash carried on without them. One pretty 24-year-old was crestfallen: 'That Jason is so gorgeous. I was just working up the courage to go up and ask him for a date when suddenly he and the others were whisked away.'

When they played Manchester the band could hardly contain their happiness and pride. The local lads had made it in a big way.

'That was the one when our parents turned up to see the show,' remembered Mark. 'Though they had seen us on TV and doing little personal appearances at clubs, they had never seen us do a big show like that. It was a very special moment both for them and for us. They were all there. I remember now before we went on, we were all really nervous because that show meant so much to us. That was a really wonderful night.'

'We did two shows at Manchester's Apollo,' said Gary. 'Originally when I spoke to my mum about coming to the show, she said she would just come on the one day. But the next morning after the show she was on the phone, saying how much she had enjoyed it and that she would love to come again. That made me feel so good.'

There were all kinds of scrapes, scraps and suffering throughout their tour. In 'Give Good Feeling' there is a fight sequence and one night Robbie put his finger in Jason's nipple ring by accident and ripped it out. 'It started bleeding and it was really painful,' complained Jason.

'Jason kept kicking me in the fight sequence,' Robbie defended himself. 'And he wasn't pretending to kick me. He was doing it for real. He got really carried away.'

Mark admitted that though the dance 'fights' they do on stage are imitation, now and again things do go over the top and they end up with black eyes and cuts and bruises.

'And it's not just the band that get carried away,'

said Robbie. 'The fans watching us do too.' One of the things they throw are dummies. And a dummy travelling at full speed is like a flying bullet. 'I nearly got knocked over by one during our performance.' It's not just dummies that their adoring fans throw – there are chocolates, paper planes and cuddly toys, as well as undies and love notes.

Every town during that tour which was to change their lives for ever brought back memories. Mark has particularly fond recollections of York, the final date in the tour: 'When we started the last song of the show, "Take That and Party", the fans went mad. They began bombarding us with teddy bears. There must have been about two hundred thrown on stage that particular night. It was quite amazing. And those bears all found a good home – after each show we give all the presents to a local children's charity to help children who haven't got many toys.'

After the tour finished, the band nursed those parts of their bodies that had come in for the worst punishment: 'Our ears were really ringing and our knees were aching,' said Howard. 'After the tour I don't think my knees would have been able to take much more. They were absolutely black and blue – even though I had been using knee pads as protection the whole time. That shows just how much punishment they took.'

Gary summed things up: 'We were exhausted and knackered, but very, very happy. Performing in front of those fans was absolutely electric.'

During rehearsals, when nothing seemed to be going right, the band had got together and said a prayer. At the end of the triumphant tour they gathered in their dressing room and thanked God for their success – for Take That, there was no doubt that their prayer had been answered.

GARY BARLOW

'One day I'd like to be a pop star'

There were never any doubts that Gary Barlow would grow up to be a musician.

At the tender age of thirteen the musical prodigy was already writing his own songs and performing around Britain in a band.

He was soon earning £140 a week, an incredible sum for a youngster. And by the time he was fifteen, Gary had already written some of the songs that would one day top the charts for Take That, including 'A Million Love Songs' and 'Why Can't I Wake Up With You'.

Gary was just twelve years old when he landed his first job at a club in Connah's Quay, North Wales. 'I performed at a talent show there, playing the keyboard,' says Gary. 'I didn't win, but after my performance the secretary at the club asked me if I wanted a job there! And naturally I jumped at the chance. I remember when I first went up on stage to play my songs my hands were shaking,

The Take That Fact File

but as soon as I touched the keyboard everything was OK.'

Gary played at the club for two years and acquired himself quite a reputation in the local area. 'I would play the organ every Saturday night for £18 an evening. It was great fun, and it was a wonderful start.'

The next musical venue for Gary was a club in the prosperous Cheshire town of Runcorn. 'In North Wales I was performing just on my own, but when I went to the club in Runcorn I had a bass player and a drummer. I considered it a move upwards,' says Gary. 'It was a very popular club and a great place for breaking new talent. Among the acts that performed there were people like Bobby Davro.

'I played there for about three years and really enjoyed it – though of course it was very far removed from the life of a pop star. I was doing cover versions while people all around me were smoking, drinking and eating chicken in a basket. But it was wonderful training – the guys in the band I was playing with were in their mid fifties, and they taught me not only a lot about music, but a lot about life, too. They were my musician years, if you like, I learned so much in them. It was while I was playing the club that I realized I wanted to be a musician more than anything else. And I was making a lot of money too, for a schoolboy. It was as if I had struck gold.'

Throughout this time Gary was hard at work on his song-writing. 'I used to love writing songs,' he admits. 'Sometimes I would set myself the task of writing one song a day. Very often ten hours is all it would take me to write and record the whole song.' But he would very rarely draw on his own experiences for his inspiration. 'I have to say that most of my songs are written about other people's experiences and not my own – though I would never dream of telling my friends that the song is about them! When you're trying to write something from your own experience, you only get your own selfish angle. When you're looking at someone else's problems, I find that you get a much better overall view.'

He says of Take That's hit 'Why Can't I Wake Up With You': 'I wrote that back in 1987 when I was about sixteen. It was written around the same time as "Never Want to Let You Go", though it has had a few readjustments since then.'

Despite the long hours that he would devote to his musical career each week, Gary still managed to do very well at Frodsham High School. When he left the school, where his mum, Marjorie, was a teacher, he had six O levels under his belt. 'I think it was easier at school to get on with your work, than not to get on with it,' says Gary. 'If you didn't, you got hassles from the teacher – especially when your mum worked there. So I just got on with it.

'Obviously there were times when I felt really knackered – like when I had come home from a club at two in the morning and had to go to school the next day. But all in all it worked out great.'

It wasn't just Gary's mum who was aware of his prodigious musical talent, the other teachers were, too. As a young boy Gary loved to test out his compositions on the staff and students before going off to local clubs to play.

Head teacher Robin Browne recalls: 'Gary's first love was music and from a young age he had a certain star quality and stage presence. He often performed in school concerts and always appeared confident at what he did, though I imagine at times he must have felt nervous.'

While Gary was at Frodsham High School he proved he had extraordinary talent by winning two national music competitions. 'After Gary won the competitions it gave him more confidence in his musical abilities and he got a lot of good advice from the judges,' says Mr Browne. 'I'm not surprised at his success but I am surprised at how quickly it has happened.'

Gary always received a lot of support from the staff and pupils. 'I remember Gary used to come and talk to me about his music, and he even gave me some of his tapes to listen to. From an early age he was serious about a music career,' says Mr Browne.

And while Gary excelled at music and put in extra hours on the piano stool he did not let his other school work suffer. 'Gary definitely stood out when it came to music but he did not let it get in the way of his school work. He was always a very popular student. And by the time he got to the fifth form he was already starting to gather fans around him, including a number of female admirers.'

Adds Mr Browne: 'He has visited the school from time to time to say hello but it has always been quite low key. I would love him to come back and perform here but I imagine it would be difficult now with all the fan hysteria.'

Gary's parents, Dad Colin and Mum Marjorie, were another constant source of support. 'They were very understanding,' says Gary. 'Of course they wanted me to do well at school, but they knew my heart was set on making music. They were great because they really let me do what I wanted to do and I am the sort of person who when they want to do something will do it. Ever since I was twelve I have directed my own life, and they never got in my way and had the utmost faith in me. I will always be grateful for that.'

But Gary's parents had some worries about the pop world, where even outstanding talent does not guarantee success or a livelihood. At one time Gary's mum wanted her son to be a policeman. 'She thought that would be a great job for Gary,' laughs the band's manager, Nigel. 'Could you just imagine him a policeman? You never know if the coppers are joking or not when they talk to you, and that's just the way Gary is.'

'My mum did want me to be a policeman,' admits Gary, 'until she got fined one day for speeding and then she cooled on the idea! I don't know why she wanted me to be a policeman. Maybe she thought I was trustworthy. Certainly I'm very strong-minded and know exactly what I want.'

So far Gary is the only member of the band to have purchased his own home, a pretty house in the picturesque Cheshire countryside. Gary has been able to splash out because he receives royalties every time anybody buys a copy of a record he has written, so earns more than the other members of Take That.

'I love living out in the countryside. My house is completely detached – the nearest neighbour is around two hundred yards away,' says Gary. 'And that is nice. The life I lead is so hectic that it's good to be able to go somewhere where you can relax, far away from it all. It's very green where I am, but not too far from Manchester, so if I need to get there for something important it's no hassle. I love that area, it's where I grew up. I know a lot of pop stars live in London when they make it, but I don't fancy that. I want to stay close to my roots.

'And I don't have to travel far to work. I have built my own recording studio in my home which means whenever inspiration strikes I can put a song down on tape without too much trouble.'

Gary doesn't see why the fact that he earns more money than the rest of the band should cause problems or jealousies. 'Basically there is no difference between me and the other guys. We all have different talents. I just have a knack for song-writing. Yes, I do make more money than the others because of my writing but all the lads understand that. That's just the way it works.'

When 'Could It Be Magic', the dance version they did of Barry Manilow's 1978 hit, reached number three in the charts and became their biggest hit to date, Gary defended the band's choice to do yet another cover version: 'I don't mind doing anything, I must admit, because I'm always willing to try something new. I'm not a precious kind of song-writer. I don't think that every hit we have should be one of my own songs. I think it is good for the band to do other people's songs. Besides, cover versions are part of today's music. They introduce kids to music that they haven't heard before.

'I thought that the obvious next single off the album was "Could It Be Magic". I know record companies like new acts to do cover versions because they can often be a safe way to have a hit. I know they have talked about us doing some more and it's all right with me. So long as the records are brilliant and they're hits, I don't care what we release!'

MARK OWEN

'I prayed and prayed'

Mark Owen is the 'cutest' Take That star, say their legions of fans. He regularly sweeps pop polls in the 'Most Fanciable Male' and 'Most Kissable Lips' categories. It is not hard to see why – he has flawless skin, bright, white teeth and sky-blue eyes. Standing just 5 foot 7 inches, he is more like the fresh-faced boy next door than any of the others.

Mark, like Robbie, was a born actor, but unlike Robbie he always dreamed of a pop career. At the age of four he already had a pop idol – the most famous rock star in history – Elvis Presley. Mark's mother, Mary, has always been an avid Elvis fan – and it was a case of like mother, like son. Mark, who was born Mark Anthony Owen on 27 January 1974 in Oldham, Lancashire, says: 'I've always liked to entertain. I think that from the minute I could walk I was doing Elvis impersonations in front of the mirror. My mum had hundreds of Elvis records and she drilled her love of Elvis into me.'

Mark's sister Tracy also caught the Elvis bug.

Mark recalls: 'We used to brush our hair back, put on blue suede shoes and tight trousers, and take a tape recorder into the street outside our home where we would both do Elvis impersonations. We would put on mum's Elvis tapes and sing and dance along to them for anybody walking by. That was the first time I ever performed for anybody, but since then I've been hooked.'

At school, Oldham's St Augustine's, Mark was a member of the choir and a regular in plays. 'I always loved acting,' he says. 'I think I must have upset some of the older pupils at school because though I was younger than them I was always getting the big parts – the parts that the older guys thought they should get.' He had to put up with some teasing from his classmates, especially when his voice started to break while he was playing the role of Jesus. 'Everyone was going around taking the mickey out of me because my speeches were turning into high pitched squeals. It was so embarrassing,' admits Mark.

As well as a love for entertaining, Mark also had a talent for sport, especially football which he was completely crazy about. He was a member of a local team called Freehold Athletic and became one of their outstanding players, winning the player's player of the year award. One of his most cherished memories of that period was scoring a hat trick during a cup final match. 'That day will stay with me for as long as I live,' says Mark, who played mainly in the midfield. 'It was like a dream come true.'

As a young teenager Mark's ambition was not to be an entertainer but to be a professional footballer. He had trials for one of Britain's greatest football clubs, Manchester United, as well as for nearby team Rochdale, but they came to nothing. Then a groin injury scuppered any chance of a career in football. 'That was one of the worst days in my life,' recalls Mark. 'I was completely shattered. I had really set my heart on becoming a professional.'

His love of sport didn't interfere with his school work and when he eventually left he had six O levels to his credit. German, Mark's worst subject, was not one of them. During one German exam he scored a measly 13 per cent, his lowest mark ever!

Mark is remembered fondly by school staff. Teacher John Fairfoull recalls him as a cheeky eleven-year-old on an adventure holiday in Tenby, and how the youngsters talked their way into entering a nightclub even though they were very under age. 'We took them out for the evening and we left them for an hour in the arcade and told them they were to meet us at the minibus. But at the allotted time there was no sign of the group. We eventually found them at the local nightclub where they had somehow managed to persuade the bouncers to let them in.'

Like the other teachers, Mr Fairfoull did not expect Mark to be a pop star. 'I don't remember him being into music while he was at school. All I do remember is that he loved football.'

That is a verdict echoed by Mark's careers teacher, Fred Laughton. 'I can't remember him showing any signs of being keen on music, singing or dancing, though I can remember his younger sister Tracy used to sing beautifully at school shows. Mark was very good at soccer though he was a little bit of a poser; he used to prepare his looks and comb his hair before and after he went on the football pitch.' It was Mr Laughton who thought Mark might have a future in banking, when Mark went to see him about his career prospects. 'Mark came to me with the idea of wanting to work in a bank and we went from there. At the time I thought it might suit him because he was a personable sort of chap and I thought he would be good with the public.'

While he was still at school Mark decided to

launch himself into the music business. He got an after school job at Manchester's Strawberry Studios where he did all kinds of tasks – including making the tea! One day he walked into the studio where Gary was recording his songs and, though they didn't know it at the time, the beginnings of Take That were born. Mark would sing the songs that Gary was writing, and the two of them decided to join forces and form a band which they called The Cutest Rush. 'The songs were good,' says Gary, 'and we made some early demos, but we never played any dates as such.'

A band can't survive on dreams alone and after Mark left school he knew he had to find work. His mum was keen for him to get a job in the bank, but for a while he worked in a trendy Oldham boutique, Zuttis. Maggie Hughes of Zuttis remembers him well. 'He got the job when he walked into the shop one day and asked if there was any kind of work. He said he was quite happy to do anything at all and he didn't mind just as long as he could earn some money. He was really nice and he had a big, beaming, bubbling smile on his face. He was always so enthusiastic, we were very taken by his personality and his manners. He didn't just impress us, he won over quite a few girls too. I remember he had lots of female admirers while he was working here. That was not only because he was so cute and good-looking but also because he was such a warm person.

'Even after he left us – and we were very sad to see him go – to work in the bank, he always came to help us out at weekends and on Sundays, whenever we needed someone. He was very obliging, a natural salesman, and people took to him because he was so pleasant. He was charming without being false. And he was a very hard worker – he always came to work before the official time and he was always prepared to stay late.

'Mark really loved music and clothes. He was always the one who put tapes on in the shop. Sometimes he would even dance to them. He was very fashion conscious. Most of the money he was paid went on buying clothes, and he always picked the trendiest stuff in our shop. He particularly liked dark colours, black and navy. He still loves clothes and enjoys trying new fashions as they come along.

'We were all thrilled when he told us he had joined Take That. It was a big thing for him to leave the safety of a secure job at the bank, but he was prepared to take that chance. I remember we made him one of the first pairs of trousers that he ever wore on stage – see-through, baggy, black nylon – which I think he wore at a gig in Scotland. They were pretty risqué.'

The two are still good friends. 'Mark comes in the shop quite often,' says Maggie. 'A few Saturdays ago some fans arrived while he was in the changing rooms. It's lucky they didn't see him actually changing, they would have fainted. When his fans come in they leave posters, CDs and records for him to sign and he always obliges. He thinks the world of his fans. I can honestly say stardom hasn't changed him a bit. He's just as nice and normal a person as he always was.'

Mark admits that he really didn't know what job to go for when he left school. 'I worked in Zuttis, I worked as an electrician's mate and I also worked in the local Barclays Bank. I basically did bits of everything just to get some money. I did all right at school and came out with some good results but by that time I had already met Gary and I wanted desperately to do something in music. That was my real interest and I prayed and prayed that one day I would be able to do it for a living. I didn't even care if all I did at the beginning was carry Gary's equipment around. I just wanted to be part of the music world.'

His prayer was eventually to be answered – though his mum, who was so thrilled about her son getting a job in the bank, was not thrilled about him embarking on a pop career. 'Yes, my mum was wary about me becoming part of a pop group at first,' says Mark. 'But once she had a talk with Nigel and he convinced her that we did have a future, she felt much better about it. Now I think she gets more excited than most of our fans when she goes to shows. She loves the band and our music.'

Mark's success in winning the pop polls so regularly gets him a lot of playful ribbing from the other band members, who enjoy teasing each other and deflating any member's ego that gets too out of hand. 'The rest of the band call me "cute" but I don't think I am,' protests Mark. 'If I was over six foot tall they wouldn't say that about me. And maybe being cute is OK when you are young but I don't want to be called that for the rest of my life.'

It was that cuteness that resulted in the band's security being stepped up after a number of their fans said they wanted to 'kidnap' him. Mark admits: 'Some of the grownup fans quite frighten me. Especially when they get so carried away. They start off by just wanting your autograph and the next thing you know they are trying to eat half your face.'

It was Jason who turned Mark on to vegetarianism. Mark knows how important it is to keep fit and healthy in a world where you are working all hours of the day and night, seven days a week. 'I take multi vitamin tablets every single day. I find that ensures I get every supplement and vitamin I need. But I don't really like to preach about healthy eating. I'm not saying that what I take everybody should take. I think it's each to his own belief. And this is what I feel I need to keep me healthy.'

So busy is the band's schedule, Mark celebrated his last birthday in a Stockholm disco, but he didn't mind too much. 'My birthday was fun, even though it happened in a place thousands of miles away from Manchester and after a hectic day's promotion. We had a meal in a Thai restaurant and then we went to a great Stockholm hangout called Café Opera for some dancing and a little drink. But it was only a little one. Even though it was my birthday I, like the other guys, had to be in bed by twelve thirty.'

The blond-haired star, who lists his favourite bands as the Waterboys and UB 40, says that just like the rest of the band he gets incredibly starstruck when they meet up with famous pop stars. 'We are still very much in awe when we meet people. We've met Annie Lennox and Lionel Richie and I bet to a partner we were all embarrassed about asking them if it was OK to get our picture taken with them. We were all dead nervous. Meeting up with Status Quo was also great fun. I think it's important to meet other pop stars because you can learn so much from them. Status Quo have been in the business for thirty years, so they've got to be something special. They know all the ins and outs of it. What we all liked so much about them was just how friendly and down-to-earth they were. Though they have been in the business all that time and we, compared to them, are complete newcomers, they treated us with respect and that really knocked us out. They weren't at all like big shots looking down on us as just a bunch of kids. They couldn't have been warmer and more encouraging. They were really nice geezers and I'm sure that's one of the reasons they have survived in this business so long.'

Mark's musical tastes also gave the name to his pet lizard, called Nirvana after the American grunge rockers. 'I thought my lizard had died because he hadn't moved a single centimetre for hours. Then I put on a Nirvana record and he suddenly came to life. He's a great pet to have but I hope he doesn't become too much of a problem.

He's eighteen inches tall already and I have been told he will grow to over three feet.

'The other day my mum got in a real state because she thought she had killed him by spraying him with furniture polish. She usually sprays Nirvana with water but she was cleaning my bedroom at the time and picked up the wrong spray by mistake. After a few minutes the lizard, which is green, turned a ghastly shade of white and then started scuttling around the cage in a mad fit. My mum was dead upset, she thought he was about to die. Luckily the next day he had turned back to green and was in his usual dozy state.'

Mark understands that the band's hectic schedule means that sometimes friendships suffer. 'You can't really lead a normal life,' he admits. 'It's hard to see all your friends because we are away so much of the time but if they are real friends they understand all that.'

Mark, who claims one of his ambitions is to be taller, reckons he is the quietest member of the band. But when he gets on to a subject that interests him, he admits that he 'can natter on all day'. His quiet image also evaporates quickly when he does his party trick . . . when the mood takes him he leaps on to the nearest table and does those hip-grinding Elvis impersonations that he first did when he was a five-year-old boy.

Mark is sometimes teased by the other band members for being a 'mummy's boy', and while he and his mum had their fair share of disagreements when Mark decided to pursue his pop career seriously, he admits that they are very close. Like most mothers, Mary Owen had a great deal of reservations to overcome about her son getting involved with a pop group, but Mark would not be put off and repeatedly assured her that 'things would be all right'.

He got it slightly wrong. Things for Mark Owen have not only been all right, they have been awesome.

HOWARD DONALD

'I don't think I'm that handsome'

It's little wonder that Howard Donald can dance and sing so well, for performing is in his blood. Both his parents are very musical: his father was a Latin American dance teacher while his mother was a talented singer who once auditioned for the prestigious Hallé orchestra.

Howard, who is the oldest member of the group – he was born in Manchester on 27 April 1970 – definitely believes their talent has rubbed off on him. In an interview he did with me just after the band had finished their spectacular first British tour, brown-haired Howard, whose muscular frame earned him the nickname of Centrefold, admitted: 'I never knew I would be doing something like this, but I should have been prepared for it because my parents are both very musical. I guess I must have got my dancing ability from my father who earned a lot of medals for his dancing.'

Howard is the most reserved member of the group though behind his brooding good looks lies

a boy who likes having fun. He admits that at
school he was always the class prankster who was
popular with his mates because he made them
laugh. His clowning and joking could be the reason
why he left school without an O level to his name.
'I wasn't too bothered about exams and that kind
of thing. I preferred to make people laugh, that
gave me a great buzz. I was a bit of a fool really.'

Sometimes Howard would bunk off school and
spend his free time in the Lancashire countryside
doing back-flips and somersaults – he excelled at
acrobatics. If school could be one long gym lesson,
he thought, then I could enjoy it. But school wasn't
and Howard hated being cooped up in a stuffy
classroom. Once he bunked off school for five
weeks in a row. 'I only intended to have a few
days off,' he says, 'but I kept taking another day,
then another day, till the days had run into weeks.
I got into awful big trouble over that.'

When Howard left school he got on to a YTS
scheme, like his friend Jason Orange. Unemploy-
ment and the recession had bitten hard in the area
that Howard had grown up in and he grabbed the
chance of a job with open arms. He became a
vehicle painter for which he earned the princely
sum of £40 per week.

'It was a way of earning a little bit of money,'

remembers Howard, 'but in the end I got fed up with coming home with a face covered in red paint.'

Clubbing had always been a way for Howard to cope with the boredom of school and later the boredom of work. As a teenager he would spend a lot of nights in the local Manchester clubs, dancing to his favourite records, and the other club goers couldn't fail to notice that here was someone who could hold his own with Michael Jackson when it came to fleet-footed dance steps. Howard was already part of a break-dance troupe called the RDS Royals. One of their biggest rivals on the break circuit was a group called Street Machine, featuring a dancer called Jason Orange.

It was while break-dancing at Manchester's Apollo club that the dance paths of Howard and Jason became entwined. 'I was a regular down at the Apollo,' says Howard. 'I used to go there with a friend called Russell, and that was where I first got talking to Jason. He was in this dance crew group. We got on really well. I loved his dancing and we decided to hook up together.'

Soon Howard discovered that dancing didn't only make him feel great, it could also earn him money. He and Jason began performing their break-dance routines together and called themselves Street Beat. They were a great success and they soon found they were earning £25 a night for a show. It wasn't enough to buy a luxury mansion with, but it was a start.

Howard also found himself dancing on television, on a most unlikely programme – *Come Dancing*!

Come Dancing is a British TV institution and its mainstays are the quickstep, the waltz and the tango. In recent years, though, an offbeat section with more modern dance has been introduced and it was here that Howard found success performing an incredibly acrobatic version of some tunes from the great Hollywood musical of the fifties *Seven Brides For Seven Brothers*. The musical tells the story of a family of seven American frontiersmen who are tamed by seven beautiful women, and Howard strutted his stuff dressed in Wild West gear. His dancing and that of his team-mates went down a storm and they managed to win their section. 'I got involved with them because they saw how good at break-dancing I was and wanted something a little off the wall for the number they were going to do,' says Howard. 'And though I have always been into break-dancing, I'm also very much into choreography and love making up routines. I think that appealed to them too.'

Together with Jason, Howard is the man responsible for devising the band's sexy bump and grind routines and the one who drives the girls wild when he tears off his shirt to reveal the well-honed physique that he keeps in shape with hours of gruelling gymnastic work and a very healthy diet, usually kick-started every morning with a bowl of muesli, egg on toast and orange juice.

Howard's views can vary according to the mood he's in. Sometimes when he feels loud, he admits, 'If you've got a good body you should flaunt it,' while at other times the modest man inside him confesses: 'If a girl says I have a nice body, I go quite shy. I don't think I'm that handsome.'

The pranks and hoaxes that he perfected at school have now found their way into the band's life and they liven up the days when the pressures of their success, as well as their gruelling work schedules, threaten to get the better of the boys. One piece of mischief that is talked of to this day is the time Howard laced Mark's codpiece with itching powder. 'I have never seen anyone dance so fast in all my life. Not even Michael Jackson,' laughs Howard, who votes Michael Jackson as the superstar he would most like to meet.

Though he is often shy and modest in interviews, one topic that is guaranteed to get Howard fired up is the comparison of the band to American teen idols New Kids on the Block. The New Kids dominated the pop world in the late eighties, enjoying a string of hits all over the world. There are many comparisons for the critics to latch on to: both bands have five good-looking guys in them, both bands feature breath-taking dance skills and both bands drive female fans crazy with their romantic songs, stunning looks and 'strip' routines. Howard got sick of hearing about the New Kids at a very early stage: 'All those comparisons are ridiculous. If you saw us on stage, you would see the difference. Our routines are much tighter and much more varied.' He also reacted strongly to suggestions that the band were cynically manufactured and hyped. 'People who say that don't really know what we're about. We write more of our own material and we do our own choreography. We're in control when it comes to our music and our look. We always want to keep our ideas and songs fresh – that's important for us if we want to keep moving ahead.'

When Howard was offered the job in Take That his mum, like most of the other parents, was concerned. 'She was worried it was just a pipe dream that would never amount to anything,' says Howard. 'I felt a bit bad at first, too, because when

I was doing my vehicle painting job I was giving Mum a regular amount of money every week. When the band started I did a few odd jobs but they didn't bring in enough money to be able to pay for my keep. So I was basically giving mum nothing.' To his relief, this isn't a problem he has to worry about any more.

Howard has suffered a series of injuries thanks to the band's exhilarating, often dangerous, dance routines. On one occasion the dance steps were so hot they burnt his feet – literally! 'We were doing a summer road show and like an idiot I decided to take my shoes off. What I hadn't reckoned with was that we were dancing on a metallic floor which got hotter and hotter as the sun beat down on it. I didn't feel any pain because I was so engrossed with what I was doing, but at the end of the show I was in real pain. The soles of my feet were burnt and covered with blisters.' But potentially his most lethal accident happened before the band was formed when he was involved in a car crash. 'I had only been driving for about six months,' recalls Howard. 'I was on a dual carriageway with a friend and it was pouring with rain. All of a sudden, two of the cars in front of me slowed down and I slammed on my brakes to avoid hitting them. It didn't work. Because it was so wet I skidded completely out of control and smashed into the car in front, while my back end hit another car. I caused a five-car pile-up. All these women got out of the cars sobbing their eyes out. I couldn't believe what had happened. I sat in my car, paralysed, not knowing what to say or what to do. It was a nightmare. But, thank God, miraculously no one was hurt.'

Howard, who like Mark and Robbie still lives at home, understands why groups turn to drugs. 'I think one of the reasons is because there is so much pressure and so much work. Groups think drugs might help them cope. But it's a false belief. In the end they wreck your life. We have never taken them and we never would.'

Out of all the Take That members, Howard is the one who has the most trouble getting up in the morning. He says: 'I remember when I used to have to be somewhere in the morning by eight thirty, I would never wake up until eight thirty. I can't help it, I love my bed.'

The band's manager has invented his own ruse to solve Howard's sleepyheadedness. Says Nigel: 'Whenever they are staying overnight at a hotel, I will always put a phone call down to reception to ask what time Howard has booked his wake-up call for. It is always about one-and-a-half hours later than the rest of the band, so I tell them to make sure they wake him up one-and-a-half hours earlier than he wants. It's the only way we can get him out of bed.'

JASON ORANGE

'I wanted to be a dancer'

Jason Orange owes his big break to a friend's girl-friend. She realized what a fantastic dancer he was and decided that his talent shouldn't be hidden from the world.

One night after watching Jason and his best friend Neil McCartney holding court on the dance floor of a local Manchester club, she wrote a letter to the TV programme *The Hitman and Her* telling them all about him. Jason knew nothing about it till he received a note from the show asking him to come and try out for an audition, but soon he was showing his fancy footwork in front of the millions who watched the programme every Saturday night.

Jason says: 'I owe her so much thanks for that. She used to come and watch us dance all the time and thought we were brilliant. She would get dead excited about the routines we did. She was a big fan of the *Hitman* show and one day she decided to write to them.

'When I got the letter from them asking us to come up for an audition it was like a bolt out of the blue. But I knew it was a wonderful chance. I was very nervous about the audition but we did fine and they asked us to be on the programme. Those were great days. I had a lot of fun.'

Jason comes from a big family, whose parents divorced when he was young. He has an identical twin brother, Justin, an older brother, Simon, three younger brothers, Dominic, Sam and Oliver, and two half-sisters. His mother works in a doctor's surgery and his father is a bus driver. At school he was shy and retiring. 'I never joined in class discussions or put forward my point of view,' he admits. 'It was as if I was enclosed in a kind of shell.'

Jason's twin brother Justin was born just twenty minutes after him. The two of them have an incredible communication, which sometimes borders on the psychic. When they were growing up they would laugh and cry at the same kind of things, and often intuitively knew what the other was doing, even if they were miles apart. They looked incredibly like each other – before Jason grew his goatee beard – which resulted in them always getting mistaken for each other.

Their identical looks got Jason into plenty of

trouble during his teenage years from jealous boy-friends. 'Girlwise he was ahead of me,' remembers Jason. 'He used to chat up or romance other guys' girlfriends and they would come up after me or give me a beating because they thought I was him.'

Jason was not a brilliant scholar and, like Howard, with whom he does the band's choreography, he lived for dancing. He would spend as much of his spare time as he could dreaming up new routines in the Manchester clubs for his dance group the Street Machine.

When he left school, also like Howard, he joined a YTS scheme and trained as a painter and decorator. 'I worked for the local Manchester council, for their Direct Works Department,' said Jason. 'For some reason they decided to take me on to do a full apprenticeship and I worked there for about four years. I was pretty lucky to have a job, because a lot of my friends just couldn't get one, no matter how much they tried. Times were tough. I enjoyed a lot of the work. One of the things I liked about it was that it was a trade and I realized that it was very important to get a good trade behind you. Something that you could always use.'

Jason mainly painted council houses, both the inside and the outside, though more often than not he ended up outside: 'They used to throw me outside all the time because I was a cheeky git to the foreman. Standing outside in the freezing cold in the winter to burn all the paint off the window-sills was one of the worst jobs you could ever do, and it was their way of pushing people. I used to get that all the time.'

Despite his cheek, the other workers liked Jason and Jason liked the job. There were a lot of fun moments and a lot of mishaps too. 'I've dropped a few pots of paint on a few floors, and fallen off a few ladders too,' remembers Jason. 'The worst accident I was involved in was one where I very nearly burned a house down. I had been asked to burn the paint off a door of a shed in a yard. When it got to brew time, I left all the gear in the shed and went off with the other guys for a cup of tea. When I got back I opened the door and the shed was on fire! I don't know how it happened. Luckily there was nothing inflammable in the shed and I desperately ran around looking for water to put the fire out. I felt like a right plonker, though I managed to put the fire out quite quickly. But it could have been nasty. If I had spent a little longer drinking tea, the house could well have burned down.'

While working as a painter and decorator, Jason spent more and more time dancing. His first dance partner was Neil McCartney, who was part of the break-dancing troupe, Street Machine. He had also met up with Howard Donald in a local Manchester club and worked out a few routines with him.

It was while Jason and Neil were dancing on *The Hitman and Her* that their paths first crossed with that of Nigel Martin-Smith. At that time, Nigel was dreaming about forming the perfect teenage band. He had already sized up Gary Barlow and was now looking for four other guys. At first Jason just wasn't interested in Nigel's plan. Nigel recalls the occasion: 'I was down at the *Hitman* on the show with another act of mine, Damien, who was enjoying a big hit with "Timewarp", a number from the *Rocky Horror Music Show*. Jason's friend Neil approached me and told me they were looking for a manager. I wasn't really interested in Neil but I was in Jason. I thought he had a lot of star quality. But it was funny because Jason didn't really want to know about being in a pop group. He was quite happy being a dancer and wasn't bothered about anything else. I couldn't believe how dead cool he was.'

Jason himself adds: 'I was young then, young and daft. I was enjoying myself. And I just wanted to carry on enjoying myself.'

Nevertheless, Nigel eventually managed to convince Jason that his brilliant dancing could be an essential ingredient in the group he was forming. Though many of the mums were wary for their boys, Jason's mum wasn't – she was happy for Jason to join the band. As we sit talking in a plush boardroom on the sixth floor of their record company's office in Putney, Southwest London, Jason says: 'My mum was happy with anything I wanted to do. She was cool. She wouldn't mind if I was on the dole as long as I was happy. She's very young minded and believes life should be about happiness and enjoyment.'

The other band members like Jason's mum, too. She could easily pass for his older sister and all the band members joke about fancying her. Says Mark: 'His mum is very young. When Jason had his picture taken alongside her she looked just like his girlfriend. All the lads think she's a bit of all right.'

Jason, quite astounded by their reaction, manages to say: 'I wish my mum could hear all the lads speaking about her like this. It would make her day.'

Although Jason's mum was keen on him joining a pop band, Jason still had serious reservations. For one thing he had a steady job in a good trade and was earning a regular wage. He sought the advice of Peter Wilson, the personnel officer at Manchester City Council Direct Works Department, before he decided to give up his job. 'Jason came to talk to me several times about whether he should leave the department or not when the opportunity arose for him to join the band,' remembers Mr Wilson. 'He was concerned that he was giving up a secure job and he knew he was taking a risk. I asked him if he had looked into everything and if he could see a future with the band and he said there was a good chance they would be a success.

'When he eventually decided to leave he was very excited and told us all to watch out for Take That. He was dead right.'

Jason had some qualms about actually passing an early audition for the band because 'before then I had only ever sung in the bath'. But he got through and quickly became a key member of Take That. He is the second oldest member of the group, born on 10 July 1970, and is the most grown-up looking with his Mohican haircut and goatee beard. Life with the band has changed his personality dramatically from the shy youngster he was at school. 'Though I do have a shy and sensitive side, these days I'm a bit of an exhibitionist. I like to be up front and speak for the band.' The other members say he is a great laugh, but they also point out what a perfectionist he is and how fastidious he can be. It is true. Jason insists on practising a dance routine till every step is absolutely perfect.

'I was totally different a year ago to what I am now,' admits Jason. 'And I know that in the next few years I am going to change more and more. Being in a band like this just can't help but change you. You meet so many people, see so many things – you can't help but learn and be influenced by everything around you.'

Jason is also the most health conscious member of the band. His diet consists of plenty of fresh fruit and vegetable juices. 'I believe that you should look after your body and because of that it's important what you put into it. I like to eat fresh food, food which is packed with vitamins. I also make sure I take plenty of cod liver oil and yeast tablets. And I have a daily drink of raw vegetable juice. It's made out of carrot, beetroot, cabbage and several other kinds of vegetables. Robbie says it smells and tastes horrible, but I love it. It does me the power of good.'

ROBBIE WILLIAMS

'I was always a bit of a joker'

Unlike the other members of Take That, Robbie Williams had no desire to be a pop star. Take That's youngest member always had a burning ambition to be an actor. From his childhood days, dark-haired, steel grey-eyed Robbie had been crazy about the movies.

His idols were movie stars, the distinguished and debonair star Cary Grant and Cockney actor Michael Caine. It was the thought of becoming a star just like them that had driven Robbie to Nigel Martin-Smith's agency in the hope of some acting work.

But Nigel had other plans for him. When he realized there was a certain something missing from the group he was putting together, he drafted Robbie in as the fifth member.

It was an irony which was not lost on the star, for when he was growing up his mum always asked him if he would like to be a pop star, the dream of so many other little boys, and Robbie always answered her 'No'. Robbie, known as the baby of the group – he was born on 13 February 1974 – told me: 'I remember very clearly watching TV when I was really young and Kajagoogoo coming on. My mum turned round to me and said, "I bet you would like to be a pop star just like them." She was quite taken aback when I told her that being a pop star didn't interest me at all, and that what I wanted to be more than anything else was an actor.'

Robbie's dream was not idle talk. 'I was entering talent competitions from the age of four or five,' he says, 'and acting from about seven years old.' But acting is one of the toughest professions to break into – as tough as pop music – and young Robbie found the going difficult at first. 'I just used to go to as many auditions as I could. At first I had no luck at all. I would get rejected for all kinds of reasons – either I was too small, too tall or the wrong shape. But I refused to be beaten. And in the end I found myself up there acting on stage. At that time I was doing dramas or musicals in local theatres close to where I lived. But it was wonderful. I adored what I was doing.'

Among the local shows that Robbie appeared in was the Hollywood musical *Chitty Chitty Bang Bang* and Charles Dickens' classic story of an orphan boy in Victorian England, *Oliver Twist*.

In *Oliver Twist* Robbie played the part of the Artful Dodger, a streetwise teenager who is Fagin's most accomplished pickpocket and who befriends Oliver Twist when the youngster joins Fagin's den of thieves. 'That's a part that a lot of stars do when they are children,' says Robbie. 'Phil Collins is just one of the people who have been the Artful Dodger during their career. It's a great part to play. I had a constant big cheeky grin on my face and my hair kept falling into my eyes. It was really long and the production people wouldn't let me get it cut. I know there are pictures of me as the Artful Dodger floating around. I think I looked pretty yucky, it would be awful if those pictures surfaced.' He also had a minor appearance in one of television's best loved soap operas, *Brookside*. So Robbie's acting career was showing definite signs of promise when fate took a different turn.

Nigel Martin-Smith had Robbie in mind as the fifth member of Take That, but first Robbie had to have yet another audition. This one was to prove the most important audition of his life. 'I sang a Jason Donovan hit, "Nothing Can Divide Us", for the audition,' says Robbie. 'I must have been OK because all the guys agreed that I should be in the band.'

Show business has always been in Robbie's blood. His dad is comedian Pete Conway, who once won the top television talent show *New Faces*, and his mum, now separated from his father, comes from a musical family. 'When our families used to get together at Christmas time or other holidays there were always singalongs and charades,' says Robbie. 'It was great fun.'

Brought up in the potteries town of Stoke-on-Trent, Robbie left St Margaret's Ward School with only two exam passes. He says of his childhood: 'My parents split up when I was young and I lived with my mum. I was always a bit of a joker at school and I guess that's why I didn't get any good exam results. I found out very early on in my schooldays that one of the keys to being popular was making the other kids laugh. So that's what I did. I was just this chubby boy who would go around pulling faces and telling jokes and I found myself with a big circle of friends.'

Robbie was known as the class joker and his pranks have passed into school legend. Teachers at St Margaret's remember him with affection. Head teacher Conrad Bannon says: 'Robbie was bright, lively and always had a smile on his face. He was the life and soul of his class. He was very popular both with his classmates and with members of staff. He wasn't shy at all, he was a real extrovert. His great love was acting and he was always performing in various school plays and productions. He also did lots of acting in local theatres.

'We are the best school in the county for music and every child who comes here has to learn a musical instrument. Robbie would have been in very musical surroundings. But I never thought he would become as famous as he is now. I never thought that was his aim in life.'

Deputy Head John Thompson remembers Robbie as a joker, but says, 'There was never any malice in the jokes he played. He liked to have fun, but he always knew where to draw the line. He livened up class lessons but never in any negative way.

'One of my strongest recollections of Robbie was when a number of children went to a Catholic retreat centre called Soli House in Stratford-on-Avon. All the children were discussing moral issues, such as poverty, and each group had to put on a little production to examine the various issues. Robbie always led everyone in the discussions and was the one who really helped organize the playlets. He was good at adlibbing and he thought very quickly.'

Robbie's athleticism in dancing showed itself

early on during his schooldays. He loved most sports, especially football, and he is an avid Port Vale supporter. He also enjoyed cricket, though it was cricket that nearly caused him to have a fatal accident while he was on holiday as a youngster. 'I was in Salisbury in South Africa where I was playing at a local cricket club,' recounts Robbie. 'I ran into the outfield to retrieve a ball that had been hit there and as I put my hand into the long grass I heard this loud hissing noise. I looked down and there was this big snake nestling by the ball. I was petrified. Afterwards, when I told the other guys in the cricket team what had happened and described the snake, they told me how poisonous it was, and how I had been lucky to get away without being bitten.'

Just like Jason and Howard, the break-dancing bug hit Robbie, too, while he was still at school. 'He always loved dancing as a child,' recalls a friend. 'Almost every Saturday for months Robbie and a gang of schoolfriends used to go break-dancing outside Potteries shopping centre in Hanley.'

Robbie has lots of different musical tastes but – like the rest of the band – he greatly admires the Pet Shop Boys, Neil Tennant and Chris Lowe. 'They were the pop stars I most wanted to meet,' says Robbie. 'I just couldn't believe it when they turned up to one of our shows. It was so brilliant talking to them. Their music is excellent. Simple pop music, but so brilliant.'

Another fave is soul singer Lionel Richie, who writes some of pop's most romantic songs, including 'Hello' and 'Dancing on the Ceiling'. 'I just love the sentiments in his songs. It makes me laugh when people say he has had his day. His Greatest Hits album just wouldn't stop selling. He will be going for years.'

Robbie's mum was the most reluctant of all the band's mothers to let her son join Take That because when he auditioned he was so young. 'I was in the fifth year at school when I auditioned for Nigel,' says Robbie. 'My mum wanted very much for me to go to college. I would have liked to go and do English and drama at sixth form college and then eventually go to university to read drama. I had dreams of being a drama teacher.'

But it was a dream that was never to be because Robbie passed his audition to become the fifth member of Take That. 'It's a day I will never forget. Not only because it was the start of a new life for me but also because looking back on it now, it was so hilarious. It was the day that I got my exam results. I went down with my friend Lee to find out how I had done and I remember how we were both petrified about opening the envelopes that contained our academic futures. What made it even worse was that everyone around us was shrieking with delight at how they had got eight O levels or nine GCSEs. All the time Lee and I were just looking at each other, not daring to open the envelope, especially now that so many of our other schoolmates were so chuffed by the results. In the end we plucked up the courage to find out how we had done. We opened them nervously and saw we both only had two passes each. We decided to drown our sorrows, went down to the off-licence, got some drinks and just sat there wondering what we were going to do with our lives – whether we should join the Foreign Legion or what.

'I had almost forgotten all about my Take That audition. I had done it about a month before and hadn't heard anything. So I was blown away when I finally arrived home and my mum said she had some good news for me. She told me Nigel had been on the phone and that I was in the group. I couldn't believe it. I felt so ecstatic. It was such an amazing turn around to the day. So Lee, me and a couple of other mates went down the offy again – this time not to commiserate but to celebrate.'

It was Robbie, the tallest member of the group at six feet one inch, who invented one of Take That's most distinctive images, the dummy. After fans saw Robbie wearing a dummy in one of the band's photographs, thousands of them followed suit and now their concerts are awash with a sea of dummies. But it was Robbie's dummy that was to worry many people who were concerned that the energetic singer might be on drugs. He was besieged by hundreds of letters from fans who were terrified that his habit of sucking dummies was evidence that he took the rave drug Ecstasy – Ecstasy users often stuff dummies in their mouths while out clubbing because the drug makes them want to chew.

In the end, Robbie asked me if I could put a message out through my *Daily Mirror* pop column, reassuring fans that he wasn't an Ecstasy user and that there was absolutely no cause for concern. He told them: 'Please don't fret. I'm not on drugs. It's just an image, I think it looks good.

'I have had a lot of frantic letters from fans who are worried that I am hooked on drugs,' admitted Robbie. 'I want to set their minds at rest. I don't take drugs and have no interest in them at all. We are a clean-living group. I know that dummies are connected with the Ecstasy scene but that's not why I have them. The story behind my dummy couldn't be more innocent. A terrible spot came up near my mouth just a few hours before I was due to do a photo shoot with the rest of the guys. I hit upon the idea of sticking a dummy in my mouth to conceal it.'

During that interview Robbie was very concerned that innocent Take That fans could find themselves under suspicion from the police because they carry dummies. 'When I went home recently I found out that the police had confiscated a lot of dummies from our fans. I meet a lot of the local girls and boys, I love chatting with them and finding out what's been happening at home. I couldn't believe it when they told me that the police had been down to where they hang out and confiscated all their dummies. They said what they were doing was drug-related. Apparently they've been doing that up and down the country.

'I was also told that the police have been going into schools and giving talks about dummies. I was told that they were telling kids that sucking a dummy can give you a buzz, but it can also dehydrate you. That's nonsense. What is upsetting is that the police could be linking me with a drug craze. And it's just not true.'

NIGEL MARTIN-SMITH

'It's a dream come true'

He could easily be mistaken for one of the group. He has short blond hair, lively blue eyes and wears the latest fashions. He is Nigel Martin-Smith and everywhere Take That go, he goes too.

But he is not Take That's secret sixth member, he is the Svengali behind them – the band's manager. He planned and plotted, schemed and sweated to create a teenage band that could take on the world. And now his dream has come true. Nigel, who owns a Manchester-based talent agency, spent years trying to get his band together. The idea for it was there two long years before Take That was formed and the idea initially came about because of a rival band – New Kids on the Block.

During the eighties the New Kids, a five-piece outfit from Boston, USA, were the biggest teen sensation in the world. Their faces were plastered all over bedroom walls from New Zealand to Norway, and their record sales were staggering. Nigel

Martin-Smith bumped into them during the making of a TV show in Britain. He was impressed by their music – a mix of rap and dance – but not by them. 'It must have been one of the first TV shows that the New Kids had done in this country,' recalls Nigel, 'and I couldn't help but feel how obnoxious they were. They seemed to be very big-headed, strutting around the studio as if they owned it.

'It had always been my obsession to put together a band of unemployed lads, make them into a group and break them. I got fed up with always seeing bands from America or from London making it and I wanted to create a Northern group. The day I saw New Kids on the Block it all suddenly gelled. There was a huge fuss over the New Kids but I was sure I could form a band which could create an equally big stir but be charming, friendly and down-to-earth at the same time. I didn't think it would be hard to find a group of talented youngsters because having an agency I knew just how much talent there was out there. What I wanted to get right was to find five guys who were all likable and not big-headed. I would like to think I have succeeded. The only part of my dream that I got wrong was the bit about "unemployed" kids – this lot were all employed!'

The band was built around the foundation block of Gary Barlow, the first member that Nigel signed to a management deal. 'Gary had an incredible amount of writing talent,' says Nigel. 'At first I took him on as a solo artist, but I realized that he would be best in a band because his interest at the time was more in the studio than anything else. I knew Mark, too, because he hung around with Gary a lot. Then Jason and Howard turned up on the scene and before I knew it I had the band that I had always dreamed of, right there smack bang in front of me.'

But there was one thing missing – a fifth member of Take That. Nigel Martin-Smith decided he needed another member as a safety measure: 'The reason I insisted on getting another member was because I thought to myself that it could be a year or two before they got off the ground – and in that time, anything could happen. Especially one member deciding to leave, which could weaken the group.

'That was the real reason, at first, that I put Robbie in. I thought that one or two of them might drop out because it takes a lot of time to make it in this business and in my experience many people do not stay the course. They leave for all kinds of reasons – because they don't like the struggle, their parents want them to get a proper job or they're disillusioned. I didn't want any of that. I wanted the band I created to survive.'

Robbie Williams was picked out as a potential fifth member for the group and was made to audition. 'I wanted to make sure we got the right guy,' says Nigel, 'so I picked the Jason Donovan song "Nothing Can Divide Us", which is one of the hardest songs in pop to sing. I did that on purpose. Robbie was quite a good singer and I wanted to see how far I could stretch him.' Of course, he came through with flying colours.

All the band have different looks, style and personality. But though much around the band was calculated and carefully planned, their image was not. 'No,' says Nigel, 'that is just a natural thing. They are all very different guys and I encouraged them to have and develop their own personalities. I didn't want them all to be clones.'

One of Nigel's hardest tasks was to persuade all the parents to let their sons pursue a pop career. When the band actually signed their contract, Nigel invited most of the parents to be there, to check that nothing underhand was happening. Says Nigel: 'The toughest mum for me was Robbie's mum because Robbie was still at school. He was a bit of a baby when he auditioned for the band. His mum is a businesswoman and quite astute. And when she came in to meet me, she fired twenty questions at me about the plan I had, the way I was going to work and the future of the band. She was the one who gave me the hardest time.'

Many of the mums were wary – but what helped convince them in the end was money. Not the money that their sons might or might not earn, but the money that Nigel was ploughing into the band. 'I remember I got all the mums together and spelt it out to them. I said – I know you are worried about this, but I have put £80,000 into this band so believe me I am just as worried. When they found out how much I had invested, they realized I meant business.'

The difficulty Nigel experienced with getting the group signed up to a record company has left him with harsh feelings about a lot of the music business. He believes many record companies aren't interested in giving the public what they want, but instead what they think the public should have. 'Too many people in the music business are worried about signing acts that are credible,' says Nigel. 'They sign up prestigious acts that their mates will approve of. So much of the music industry is pretentious. It's a real joke. That's why when people like myself and Pete Waterman come along, who believe in giving the public what they want, we rock the boat. It's the same with rave music. That is being bought in droves by kids on the street, but most of the record companies look down their nose at it because they don't think it's "musical" enough.'

Though Nigel may look like one of the band members' older brother, he acts like their father. He is loving and considerate, but also strict. He makes the rules and the band have to play by them. Most nights the lads have to be tucked up in bed by 12.30. It is one of many tough rules that Nigel has imposed, and a hard one to accept when you're 22 years old and see the world as your oyster — but it is there for a reason. 'Nigel believes in working hard,' says a friend of the band, 'and though the band is fun, this is not a game. There is an awful lot at stake. Every day there is so much to do, and he always wants the band to be at their freshest.'

The rules don't just ensure the band devote themselves totally to their career, they are also designed to keep them down-to-earth. 'At one point,' adds the friend, 'Nigel insisted that the band do all their own housework and wash all their own clothes. More than anything he wants to prevent them from getting spoilt, big-headed and developing huge egos. He wants to make sure that their feet stay firmly on the ground.'

TRUE LOVE

Take That and romance

Take That will not be able to fall in love for two years . . . on their manager's orders. And that's bad news for the millions of girl fans the band have all around the world.

The band can have flings and flirtations, but anything steady is banned by Nigel Martin-Smith. And strict and harsh as it seems, the band have agreed to say no to love for that period. The reason love is a no-go area is because the band's shrewd though charming manager believes it could be the downfall of their career. Once a band member falls in love, his girlfriend could start to mean more to him than the band, worries Nigel. He knows that separating boys from true love is as difficult a task as separating cornflakes from milk, but he is determined to succeed.

Nigel is also worried that if one of the lads falls in love and has a steady relationship, he will no longer find himself so popular with the fans and that could be damaging to the band. When it was erroneously reported that Take That had a candlelit dinner with the five-piece all-girl Aussie band Girlfriend, there was panic in the Take That camp. The item said that the two groups had met in a German hotel and they had all taken a shine to each other. The band's press officer Loretta de Souza rang me up to ask me to put an item in my *Daily Mirror* column denying that the groups were romantically linked.

There was no truth in the story and I was more than happy to say so:

Take That are completely baffled by a report that they have been out on candlelit dinner dates with Aussie all-girl fivesome Girlfriend. Says Gary Barlow, whose new single 'Why Can't I Wake Up With You', is released next month, 'It's rubbish. We were at the same hotel as they were, but we weren't even sitting at the same table. Someone obviously has a lively imagination.'

After the band got back from their promotional tour, Gary again brought the subject up in an interview. 'I was really upset about that,' he told me. 'We are with the same record company as Girlfriend in Germany and they and some of Girlfriend's people came up with the idea. They thought it was good publicity. We didn't mind meeting them as they were staying in the same hotel but when we turned up there were two photographers and we were told they wanted us to sit next to a girl each. We didn't agree to it at all. There was no way we were going to do something like that. They wanted to get some publicity by using us. It happens all the time.'

Nigel has plenty to say on the subject of girls: 'Yes, I have stopped the boys from having steady girlfriends for about two years. It has caused a lot of rumours, with some people saying it's not natural for guys of their age not to have regular girlfriends, while other people are saying they must be gay, but I stand by what I did. I have never insisted they behave like monks, but what I don't want is for them to get involved in heavy, serious relationships because there is just no room in their lives for that. They are away from home all the time now because of the pressures of their pop success and if they had a relationship that would be so hard for them to deal with. They wouldn't want to leave home and leave their girlfriends. Romance is a very powerful force and if they had serious relationships that could and most probably would become the number-one thing in their lives.'

He warned the band about the 'no girlfriends'

rule right at the very beginning. 'I told the band – if you do everything I tell you right from the start, this is exactly the way your career will go – and I showed them the plan for their future. But I believed that plan could only work if they put their serious love life on hold for two or three years. I told them that once they had really made it and they had got to a certain level then they would be able to do what they wanted. But I spelled it out to them that if they wanted a career they had to work damn hard for the next three years and give up any thoughts of a serious romance, and to be fair to them that's what they've done.

'Right from the word "go", no girlfriends or friends have ever been able to come to the shows and if they want their family to come, they have to ask me first. That just ensures that everything is kept on a very professional level.

'There's a lot of trust between me and the band and that's the way it has got to be. I've always been very open with them and they've always been very open with me – that's the way it has always worked. Everything we do is discussed in the band meetings we have each week. That's when we all sit down and I ask them if they have got anything to moan about, and they moan and tell me the things that are going wrong or the things they are not happy with and we try to sort things out. Because we discuss everything, they are just as involved in the management decisions as I am. That's the kind of relationship it has to be.'

But the real worry for those around Take That is whether the boys will be able to do without love for two years. The band believe they can and say they will stick to Nigel Martin-Smith's order.

It will be harder for some than others. The band member Nigel most worries about is Howard Donald. Howard loves the comfort, warmth and security that a steady relationship can provide and Nigel believes he is the one member who will most miss a steady girlfriend. 'Howard really needs a relationship. He's going mad because he needs to be with somebody but he knows that he can't.'

Howard himself admits it. 'That's true and that's why I can see that the rule about no girlfriends makes sense. Once I fall in love, I fall in love very deeply and I think that to be in a relationship like that and to spend so much time away from a girl would be unbearable and unfair for both of us. But the way things are now, if I was to meet the right girl I would never find out if she was the right one because I wouldn't be able to spend enough time with her.'

Gary has similar views: 'Nigel isn't forcing us

into anything. He has just made us see the sense of the fact that if we want careers we have got to keep our minds on the job. We will all have relationships one day, we know that. But even when we decide that the time is right, it won't be easy because we will be in a position where a girl could easily like us because of what we are rather than who we are. I would like to think that we are all level-headed and smart enough to see through a girl who might just want to go out with us because we are rich and famous.'

But even Gary has to admit how much he likes steady relationships and how he looks forward to marriage one day. 'I have had two main steady girlfriends,' he reveals. 'The last one was a girl called Nicky, we had been going out for about three years. I did like having steady relationships but you have to face up to the fact that they don't always last.

'I know that my first relationship ended when I came to an age where I had outgrown it. The second one broke up mainly, I think, because I was moving into a totally new life. I was starting to write songs with Mark and then we did the *Hitman* TV shows and things started to happen. I went off on another wavelength and that was that really. I see girls when I go back home all the time, but never anybody steady. I know how demanding that would be, especially with the kind of work we are doing at the moment.

'But I do eventually want to get married and have kids. I don't want the business to interfere with those plans, because I don't want to miss out too much on what I want to do in life – and that can happen when the business takes over and you are under all kinds of pressure.'

Mark Owen is the band member who rates highest with fans on the cute-o-meter. He has always been a magnet for girls. Now, though, the adulation is of the kind most men could only dream about.

He too has had a steady girlfriend, but now says, 'It would be impossible for me to keep a regular girlfriend happy and be in the band at the same time. There would be too much pressure. Your girlfriend would be upset by the fact that you just never got to see her enough, as well as getting jealous of other girl fans. I prefer to be on my own or chill out.

'You have to take it one step at a time. It would be difficult to concentrate on your music and your band – and have a girlfriend at home at the same time.'

Occasionally the lack of a regular girlfriend can cause problems, finds Mark. 'Sometimes when I get home, phone my friends and ask them if they fancy coming out for the evening I feel a bit out of place when they say they can't because they are going out with their girlfriends or they say they will but can they bring their girlfriend too. That's when it strikes you what a different kind of life you lead. But maybe tomorrow we might meet the girl of our dreams. Maybe tomorrow we might fall madly in love.'

There are some advantages: 'I enjoy the idea of all these different girls liking me. It's a great buzz,' admits Mark. 'I love the attention of the fans. But don't get us wrong, we don't go about looking to make love to anything that moves. It's not like that at all.'

Jason, too, says his attitude to girls has changed since he joined the band. 'I'm sure one day I'll have a nice family and settle down. But at the moment I am used to living like this. Though I've had girlfriends in the past they've not really been steady.'

The one member of the band whose romantic life hasn't changed is the youngest, Robbie Williams. 'I have never had a steady girlfriend,' he confesses. 'The longest I have ever been out with anybody is three weeks. Long-term relationships are not me.

'All our class were out with different people all

the time. You'd be going out with this person this week and that person the next week, and that happened all through school. When I left school I joined the band, and there was no time for a steady relationship.

'Do I miss having a relationship? I don't know. Besides, you can't really miss something you've never had.'

FAN-TASTIC

The faithful followers

Take That's army of followers are the largest and most loyal of all British fans – at the time of writing the band's fan club totalled a staggering 70,000 members.

And the adulation that they lavish on the band can get scary at times. In August 1992, three months before the band set off on their series of British concerts, they began a tour of HMV record shops. The tour had to be scrapped after the band visited a store in Manchester and were besieged by 5,000 fans. In the end the band had to be smuggled out!

The incident in Manchester was just an example of the hysteria that Take That has caused throughout Britain, and which is now spreading all over the world. Sometimes the consequences can be distressing for the band and the fans. 'We had to stop doing small clubs and personal appearances in leisure centres because it really did get too dangerous,' says Gary. 'We had a lot of trouble with the police when we were doing our signings so we decided to give up on them for a while. But we were upset when the police decided we shouldn't do any appearances because a lot of fans think it was our decision. At that time we got a lot of mail from fans asking why we cancelled, saying "without us you would be nothing". What they didn't understand was it wasn't us who called those appearances off.

'Some fans thought that we'd had enough and we didn't want to do those places, but nothing could have been further from the truth. One of the most lasting impressions I have is the story of a girl who had spent hundreds of pounds on clothes and presents and stood outside a venue for four hours, only to find that it had been called off. Our fans are wonderfully loyal and we would never do anything to upset them.'

There have been some scary moments for the band. Mark remembers one time in Bristol: 'We were leaving the leisure centre and it was really a case of us running for our lives to the van which was parked nearby. The fans were going wild, chasing madly after us. But when we got to the van, we thought we'd had it – the van was locked and there was nobody in it.

'We were badly scratched before we were saved

by our crew who bundled us into the van.'

'Another time we were doing a personal appearance in a shopping centre,' recalls Robbie, 'where the crowd, who were really close to us, got carried away. Normally I put my hand out to them and then withdraw it really quickly, but this time it didn't work. When I went to try to whisk my hand away they grabbed hold of it and they pulled me forward. I fell right into the crowd. I thought I was going to get smothered, but luckily our helpers came to the rescue.'

Another time, the band were being pursued by a hoard of fans in their home town and tried to escape by dashing into a local shopping centre – only to be thrown out by the security guards!

The band are also deluged by thousands of fan letters from girls, writing about everything under the sun. Some letters just ask for autographs, others for sex, while still others say how miserable their lives are and how they want to end it all.

'We get all sorts of fan mail,' says Mark. 'It is quite staggering. They tell us about their most private thoughts and feelings. It's quite amazing how much they open up to us. With some of those letters you really feel you know the person that is writing to you because they bare their soul.

'It's difficult, of course, to answer all the letters.

At one point we tried to answer a number of them personally but sometimes we just don't have the time to answer as many as we'd like. But our helpers sift through the letters and give us a number to read, saying if you are going to answer any this week, try your best to answer these ones.'

Take That's pretty-boy looks and athletic dance routines have won them a lot of gay fans. From the early days the band performed in gay clubs and those shows, together with the fact that no member of the band has a steady girlfriend, led to the inevitable, though wrong, rumours that the band might be gay. 'The rumours started because I've always insisted that the boys play in gay clubs,' admits Nigel. 'They are five good-looking lads so the gay clubs always offered a lot more than the straight clubs. My attitude was why not?'

Performing in gay clubs was certainly an eye-opener for Gary who admits that he – like the other guys in the band – was chatted up all the time. 'We've always done gay clubs and people always used to cheer and wolf-whistle when we'd go on stage. Before the band I didn't know anything about gay people, their views or how they lived. But now I feel I've lived a whole lot more.

'Guys would chat us up all the time and they were quite forward. They'd want to know if I was

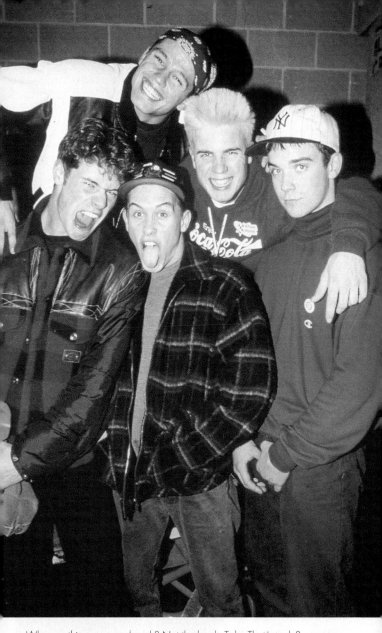

▲ Who are this gruesome bunch? Not the lovely 'Take That,' surely?

◄ 'Me take drugs? I'm no dummy,' protests Robbie

The boys look pleased with them-selves on a promotional visit to France – and so they should, with their recent chart-topping success ▼

▲ While in France the band find time to do some window shopping and a spot of sight-seeing ▼

▲ Take That get into a spin on a traditional carousel
and look set for an evening out on the town ▼

▲ The boys seem to have found themselves a helping hand...

▲ Gary takes time out for his piano practice

▲ Take That up against the wall

▲ Robbie demonstrates a cool move with a basketball

▲ You can't help but look up to five of the nicest guys in pop!

gay and when I said "I'm not" they used to say "That's cool" and keep on talking.'

The gay rumours posed no problem for any of the band members. Says Mark: 'I like gay rumours because it just creates a bit of mystery about the band. We also get a lot of letters from gay men saying they fancy us but we're not bothered by that.'

'We basically play to people who like our music,' adds Howard, 'and we just happen to have a big gay following. I don't see what's wrong with that.'

When the band decided to support AIDS charities it only strengthened the gay rumours, but they felt it was important to do their bit.

'There are a lot of important charities to support,' says Robbie, 'but AIDS is really worrying. We wanted to do this as kids often listen to us when they don't listen to teachers.'

The band are genuinely concerned for their army of fans. They know that without them they would not have the success they enjoy and they believe that too many pop stars forget that their fans are real people and instead regard them simply as a means of buying themselves the latest luxuries and maintaining their 'superstar' lifestyle.

When I interviewed Gary after their first Newcastle show, he wasn't interested in what the critics thought – he was much more eager to know whether their fans had enjoyed the performance.

He asked me: 'Did you speak to the fans last night? What were their reactions? It seemed to me like we weren't on that long. Were they moaning about how long we were on for?'

Gary and the rest of the band are determined to remain loyal to the fans who supported their pop career before they even had any chart hits.

'I love the adulation from the girls,' said Gary. 'Sometimes I wish we could get closer, sometimes I wish we could just sit and talk to them all night. I just hope that feeling never goes. I know we won't ever think we're too big time to stand and talk to them but people around us might try and pull away.'

Mark, whose boyish looks have made him the band's supreme pin-up and won him the attention of thousands of fans, adds: 'One of the main things that we have tried to ensure about the band is that we are approachable to our fans and to have constant contact with them.'

Since Take That shot to fame the fans have developed curious ways of expressing their feelings towards the band members. Mark explains: 'The fans picked up different ways of reacting to all our songs. When we were singing "Satisfied" there were Marathons and chocolate bars being thrown on stage. On "Give Good Feeling" we sing a line where we fly, fly, fly and they all made paper planes which they used to throw at us.

'And when we did a gig in York it was clear that all the fans had been planning something together. As soon as we started the last song they all bombarded us with teddy bears and streamers and spray foam. All the road crew came up on the stage and danced with us.'

Take That's fans are so hooked on the band that they will travel hundreds of miles to camp outside their homes dotted around Manchester and Cheshire. But according to Mark, some fans are more desirable than others. 'We do have both possessive fans and ones who we just see occasionally. They are all nice, although I think it's a bit unfair when we're followed everywhere by someone, especially when it's to our homes!

'That's what some of the more possessive ones do. At one point there were so many fans outside my home that I thought I should move out to give the neighbours some peace and quiet. But now I'm away from home so often, they know about it and don't come and wait outside so much. Now my dad is much happier about the state of affairs and has even been talking about selling off a few bricks from the family home as fan souvenirs! I hope he's joking.

'One of the things that constantly amazes me about the fans is how they seem to know our every move. They know when we are flying out of the country, know when we are coming back to Britain and even know what hotels we stay in.'

After Take That won an army of British fans in 1992 it looks like 1993 will be the year they conquer the world in search of more troops. And it doesn't look as if they will have any problems in attracting new recruits.

STAR CHARTS

The year ahead for Take That

Take That's astrological charts have been compiled by top astrologer to the stars Norman Plaskett, resident astrologer at London's Psychic Garden. Norman has used the Egyptian method of forecasting – the most intuitive and revealing of all.

Mark – 27 January 1974

There will be the need to deal with more than one project at a time. Mark's mind can be likened to a grasshopper with the ability to leap from one topic to another very quickly. As others will find it extremely difficult to pin him down, he may well find that they like his company, but they will not take him very seriously. There will be the opportunity to travel and meet with many strange situations on the way. Sometimes there will be the need to attempt potentially dangerous projects on a thrill-seeking level. Stimulants of all kinds are a danger and should be avoided at all costs, as there is the ability to assimilate any kind of drug extremely rapidly and thereby create the possibility of physical damage.

Dilemmas of all kinds will rear up in his path. His desires are very strong and can be overwhelming, especially within the context of his own sexuality, and consequently create confusion within the emotional life. Partners will be confused by the physical and overt approach that overlays a hardness within. To compensate for this, there will be an attitude of living for the current day, without any regard for what may transpire tomorrow.

The energy of his Chart can be used to advantage within the commercial life. There is considerable inventive potential present that will bestow the ability to invent new approaches and improve on already established methods.

Robbie – 13 February 1974

The art of synthesis is the benefit of this Chart. Robbie learns to merge his past actions with his plans for the future. There is the desire to base all his actions on strong foundations. The mind is clear and concise, with no room for ambiguous ideas or conceptions. This is the plateau of learning where power has to be tempered with wisdom.

He will show little patience for those people who are tied by hidebound concepts, and the desire to create new ways of performing old tasks is felt. There is a strong feeling of independence, and his ambitions are heightened. He will work hard to fulfil these, but if he is given a specific task to complete it is as well if he is allowed to deal with it in his own way with no interference from others.

He works quite well within a team, providing he can exercise his own individuality. Others will look to him for guidance and perhaps even place him on a pedestal. Remember that this is an extremely dangerous position in which to find ourselves, as there is only one direction open to us and that is down.

His Planets have a curious effect upon friendships. He needs them, but on his terms. It will be helpful if he remembers that we should not put people to one side when they are not required and pick them up again as the need arises.

Jason – 10 July 1970

Probably no other year will have such a radical effect on Jason's life as 1993. Its influence is all embracing, and when once he enters its sphere of influence there will probably be no area of his life that is not affected in some way. There is a reduction in his affairs that takes him back to fundamental principles, with absolutely no room for self-delusion or ambiguous attitudes. This will not be the time for half-hearted action. All has to be planned on firm foundations that will stand the test of time.

There is nothing comfortable about his Chart. All the changes that are experienced will be to some degree quite radical, but if he keeps his head and accepts opportunities as they arise, he will realize that he can now be likened to the Phoenix that rises again from the ashes of the past.

Jason will have the desire to put aside situations that have become untenable, and if this feeling is taken to extremes he may find himself cutting off his nose to spite his face. His emotional drive will be extremely strong and his actions may well be instigated by subjective impulses. Look before taking that step in the dark; there is a need to cut the ropes that bind us, but this has to be done after we have evaluated our chances of success and not before.

Gary – 20 January 1971

Gary will have a sense of completeness about his affairs, and feelings of urgency will encourage him to finish tasks as quickly as possible. He is aware that a cycle has been completed and another is yet to begin.

The influence within his Chart can be likened to the moving of home, where the old and unwanted possessions are discarded in favour of the new. There may well be news of a pregnancy or birth within his family background. Within his commercial life there will be new opportunities to take advantage of, and perhaps a new business partnership will be formed or an alliance made – if embarked upon now it will bring satisfaction to all those concerned.

Within the health pattern there will be upsets that stem from psychosomatic roots. It will be as well to remember that what goes on in the mind will manifest physically, and consequently all forms of stress and anxiety should be avoided as much as possible. This applies equally to the emotional life as well.

A relationship is needed that is indeed complete on all levels, spiritually, emotionally and physically. Without these commodities the attention will fluctuate radically between intense activity and complete disinterest. But if his partner reflects the tender and understanding facets of love there will be the realization that marriage is the full manifestation of cosmic consciousness.

Howard – 27 April 1970

The problems and requirements of others will be of prime importance. This concern results in Howard being in the position to be used beyond reasonable expectation by other people. There is a desire to be needed and some of this springs from an egocentric bias within. However, whatever his motives are, there is a strong generosity of spirit that enables him to put the interests of others before his own and, in extreme cases, before the interests of those nearest and dearest to him.

The inherent generosity within will exclude activities in a commercial world that puts money before people. If possible, business activities should include strong humanitarian or social principles.

Friendships are all-important, together with a desire to be liked by others. Some friends will remain for life and be regarded as part of his own family. He will share their joys and misfortunes gladly, and advice that they impart is taken seriously.

His Chart bestows an understanding within the emotional life. There is a preference for the long-standing relationship, rather than the affair that is short-lived. But unfortunately there is the tendency to attract the kind of partner who falls short of the same sincerity. Marriage is valued and much effort will be made to ensure that it is successful. Even if the partner should lose interest there will be loyalty to the relationship. He may tend to hang on to a relationship that no longer works, rather than go through the emotional maze of getting out of it.

ONWARDS AND UPWARDS

Current success and future plans

For Take That, 1992 ended with a string of triumphs.

In November they showed how they were dominating the British pop scene when their new single 'Could It Be Magic' reached number 3 in the charts and stayed in the Top Five throughout December. They had yet more success in December when their compilation video *Take That And Party* became the best-selling music video of 1992, even though it had only been on sale for just three weeks and was competing against videos that had been on release throughout the whole of the year. Released on 7 December 1992, the video entered the charts at number 1 and stayed there.

The band added to their run of success when they walked away with a staggering seven top prizes at the *Smash Hits* Awards. Among the prizes they picked up were Best Group, Best Single, Best LP and Best Video. The band that had been the previous year's favourites, New Kids on the Block, failed to pick up any awards. The ultimate humiliation came when New Kids' Jordan Knight had to present one of the prizes to the Manchester idols.

After the ceremony, which was screened live from London's Olympia Arena, Mark Owen told me: 'This time last year we were wondering if we'd ever make it. I can't believe this has happened to us. It's wonderful.' Later that night Take That celebrated their success at a star-studded party at L'Equipe Anglais club in London's West End where they were the toast of the night.

It was the perfect end to a triumphant year for Take That, and helped to make up for a lot of the criticism they have taken in the past. The road to fame hasn't always been an easy one for the band and they have had many harsh words written about them. One of their critics who has since changed his mind is Pete Waterman, pop mogul and presenter of *The Hitman and Her*. When Take That were struggling to win a record company deal they approached Waterman but he turned them down.

'Their version of pop music was not my version of pop music,' he says. 'I take my music very seriously and I don't believe that, at that time, they did. I found them too manufactured. But that was three years ago and they've changed a lot since then. They have had three years of working non-stop and that has really shaped them up. If they didn't have a deal and they came to me now, I would sign them up straight away.'

Gary admits he was disappointed when Waterman turned them down: 'I've always loved the Stock, Aitken and Waterman stuff. In fact, when I first started writing songs, I used to try to write mine just like theirs. So it was a bit of a blow when he said no.'

When people refused to believe in Take That it simply made the band even more determined to succeed. 'Pop music was very out when we started our career,' says Gary. 'That's why we struggled so much at the beginning. When we told people about our songs and the kind of group we were they reacted as if we were lepers. People accused us of having no talent and said we couldn't sing. I remember the first time we did *Top of the Pops* the camera crew and a lot of other production staff were having bets about whether we could even sing. But that just spurred us on. When I got up on stage at the BBC I just sang my heart out. Yes, it does make you want to try harder.'

The band spent Christmas with their families, and jetted off to Europe in the New Year to do some promotional work. Then, one cold day in January Take That received some heart-warming news. They had been nominated for two prizes – Best British Newcomers and Single of the Year – at Britain's most prestigious awards show, the BRITS, the rock equivalent of Hollywood's Oscars. The BRITS are a yearly event where the superstars of rock battle it out against each other and any act that is nominated can truly say they have arrived.

1992's BRITS were announced at one of London's most popular hangouts, the Hard Rock Café. Take That were in exalted company that day: among the nominees were such stars as Elton John, Eric Clapton, Mick Hucknall and Madonna. The band were so thrilled to be nominated that they even turned up to the restaurant that morning where they mingled with other celebrities and posed happily in front of a huge cardboard cut-out of the BRITS symbol.

At the time Robbie told me: 'I think what particularly thrilled us about being nominated for the best British newcomer award was that it is chosen by people in the music business, a lot of the big chiefs, so we were really pleased that those kinds of people were taking us seriously. For some reason people in the business seem to be more in favour of rock and indie acts, things which they see as being supposedly more serious and more credible, so getting the nomination was wonderful.'

But only a few weeks later their BRITS triumph had been shattered. Despite being nominated, the fivesome were snubbed by the organizers when they were not invited to perform at the awards ceremony. The band's reaction was understandably angry. 'I couldn't care less about the BRITS. They don't mean anything to me,' said Jason. 'People in the music industry don't seem to care about a young band like us. The awards the public vote for are the ones the bands are more interested in.'

A friend of the band said: 'I can't believe Take That won't be there. They've been one of the biggest bands of the year and the newest. The BRITS have often been criticized for being a redundant dinosaur and this is further proof. I've heard that Madness are one of the acts performing at the show. They were all right ten years ago but they're not exactly "now", are they?'

But Nigel Martin-Smith was not surprised that Take That had been left out in the cold by the organizers. 'I had a bet with the boys that they'll not win the categories they've been nominated for. I told them that they were not credible enough even though they were obviously the best newcomers. They have sold loads of records, a million singles, half a million albums. As far as I was concerned, they were the most successful act of the year. But that is one of the things that really upsets me about the business, there is so much pretentiousness in it.'

But the band did win a prize although it was one of the few awards not chosen by chiefs of the British music industry. They romped home in the Best Single category with their song 'Could It Be Magic', chosen by polling listeners of Radio 1.

Instead of going to the BRITS the band decided to take off for America. The band had conquered Britain and were ready to take on the rest of the world. Already all the signs of world domination were there. The band's records had begun selling wildly all over Europe – Germany, France, Spain and Sweden were already showing signs of full-scale fan worship.

In an interview I did with the band just after they had come back from a promotional tour of the continent they described the scenes of mass hysteria they had witnessed. Mark had even got a 'smashing' black eye from one frenzied fan. 'We came out of a TV studio in Stockholm and were mobbed by two hundred girls,' he told me. 'They just went crazy, they got so carried away, especially this one girl who whacked me in the eye with her camera. It was a total accident, she was swinging her arms around madly and hit me in the face. It hurt like anything for hours and for the next few days I was walking around with a real shiner.

'But the fans have been really great wherever we have gone. We're learning that fans are the same all over the world although our British fans will always have a special place in our hearts because they are the ones who made us. We couldn't have done it without them. We are thrilled at how well everything is going for us. We just don't know how we are going to have time to fit everything in.

'One thing we've noticed is that abroad a lot of guys have been turning up to see us. That's good. I think at the end of the day they see us over there as just a group and we should be able to have fans of all ages and of both sexes. I think that is happening here too, now.'

The band are learning to deal with spending more time abroad. When I met them after their trip to the continent, Gary had celebrated his birthday in Germany and Mark had his in Sweden. They also shot a video for their single 'Why Can't I Wake Up With You' in France. 'The video was shot about thirty miles outside Paris in an old chateau,' says Gary. 'It was gorgeous. We wanted to get a very moody feel for the video and we hope we succeeded. Actually, the place we were in – though it was nice – was very boring. We sat around for three days really doing nothing, just waiting to do our shoot. There was a moat around the chateau which was all frozen up and we used to play dare devil games and see who could walk the furthest on the lake. We were all egging each other on, but luckily no one fell in.'

'The highlight of the week was finding a dead stoat frozen up in the ice,' adds Robbie. 'We used to go and sing songs to it because that was the only interesting thing to do. It was very desolate. There was only one restaurant and that didn't have a great choice of food. We went there every night and had the same meal. If we hadn't been working there perhaps we could have taken advantage of the beauty and peacefulness of the place but so much of the time was spent just hanging around waiting to be filmed for our various scenes.' The single, 'Why Can't I Wake Up With You', was a smash success, rocketing to number 2 in the charts in the first week of its release.

Over the last few months their gruelling schedule has become even more hectic. 'It's a bit like if it's Monday it must be Spain,' laughs Gary. 'Sometimes we've been to four different countries in four days. It sounds glamorous when you read about it, but it is actually very hard work. When we went over to Germany for three days recently we started work at nine in the morning and didn't stop till midnight. But it's something we know we have to do. We're thankful that people like us so much. We realize that we could be working as hard in every country as we did in Britain. The other day I got back from somewhere or other, I can't even remember the country, and couldn't wait to jump into my bed. I fell asleep on Sunday at five in the evening and the next thing I knew the phone was ringing and it was ten minutes past four the next afternoon.'

The band are very aware that their newfound success all over the world – Europe, America and Japan – will take them away from their British fans for a while. It is something that worries them a great deal. 'We all worry about leaving England for too long,' says Gary. 'We know that it is important for us to be successful in other countries, every group has to move on, but we will certainly never desert Britain and our wonderful fans here. We have worked so hard to get them, and they have been so loyal that we don't want to do anything to disappoint them. We think about them all the time.'

Mark has similar views: 'There are far too many bands who have a few hits in Britain and then decide they've got what it takes to conquer the world and consequently leave all their old fans behind. We will never do that.'

The band practise what they preach. British fans will be able to see their Take That in all their glory this summer when they play a series of major concerts all over the country. Four dates have been announced for July, all at huge venues: Glasgow SECC on 21 July, Manchester G-Mex 22 July, Birmingham NEC 23 July and London's Wembley Arena on 24 July.

They will be the pop shows of the year and Take That want to see YOU there.

WHAT HAPPENED WHEN

1984 — Jason Orange is in a break-dance crew, Street Machine, while Howard Donald is in a crew called the RDS Royals. Later they join together to form Street Beat.

1987 — Gary Barlow meets Mark Owen at Manchester's Strawberry Studios and they eventually form a group together called The Cutest Rush.

1990 — Both groups meet through Nigel Martin-Smith's Manchester-based entertainment agency. They advertise for a fifth band member and Robbie Williams auditions and gets the job.

September 1990 — Take That formed and sign contract.

March 1991 — The band secures a slot on the BSB show *Cool Cube*.

April 1991 — The band embarks on a regional tour of British clubs.

The Take That Fact File

July 1991 – Take That's debut single, 'Do What U Like', is released on Nigel Martin-Smith's independent label, Dance UK. Single reaches number 82.

Jelly and ice cream video, co-produced by Ro Newton and Angie Smith, is shown on *The Hitman and Her*.

September 1991 – Take That sign a major album deal with RCA after head of A&R Nick Raymond hears about them and sees them perform.

October 1991 – Band undergoes a change of image, dumping the leather look for string vests.

November 1991 – The band's second single, 'Promises', is released and reaches number 38.

Take That appear on *Wogan, Going Live, O-zone, Motormouth* and *Pebble Mill*.

December 1991 to January 1992 – The band complete their LP.

January 1992 – 'Once You've Tasted Love' released. It reaches number 47.

February 1992 – Take That embark on the famous 'Safe Sex' tour, organized in conjunction with the Family

Planning Association. They perform at schools and clubs up to four times a day, along with promo signings.

May 1992 – 'It Only Takes a Minute' is released and reaches number 7. The single marks the first real success for the band.

They appear at the Children's Royal Variety Performance. Princess Margaret says backstage that she loves their saucy dance routines.

June 1992 – The band appear on the Radio 1 Road Show at Alton Towers and receive an incredible reception.

They appear at Crystal Palace for National Music Day.

August 1992 – New single, 'I Found Heaven', is released and reaches number 15.

Debut album *Take That and Party* is released and reaches number 2.

HMV record shop tour begins. Fans besiege the band in London, Glasgow, York and Manchester. HMV cancel the rest of the tour for safety reasons.

October 1992 – 'A Million Love Songs' is released, which rises to number 7.

November 1992 – UK tour begins, taking in major venues throughout Britain.

The Take That Fact File

December 1992 — The band win seven awards in the *Smash Hits* poll: Best Band in the World, Best British Band, Best LP, Best single and Best video. Mark Owen wins awards for Best Haircut and Most fanciable male.

Take That also win eight awards in *TV Hits* magazine readers' poll.

December 1992 — Take That release the video of *Take That and Party*, which rockets to the number 1 spot.

'Could It Be Magic' released, which reaches number 3 in the chart.

January 1993 — Take That nominated for two BRITS awards.

February 1993 — Take That release a new single, 'Why Can't I Wake Up With You'. It storms straight into the charts at number 2. They win Best Single category at the BRIT awards for 'Could It Be Magic'.

QUIZ

Are you a truly dedicated fan? Test yourself and see.

1 Which northern city do most of the Take That members come from?

   a) Bradford
   b) Liverpool
   c) Manchester ✓

2 He started on his first keyboard at only ten. He now writes Take That's songs. Who is he?

   Gary Barlow ✓

3 To concentrate on becoming megastars, the guys have given up romance. But for how long?

   two years ✓

4 One fan said he should do a spread for a sexy magazine, and now his nickname is 'Centrefold'. Who is he? *Howard* ✓

5 Which ballroom dancing competition did Howard's troupe win? *Come dancing* ✓

6 Who is the youngest member of the band and has the nickname 'Baby'?

Robbie Williams ✓

7 When Robbie first started sucking a dummy, what was he hiding?

(a) A spot
b) A black eye
c) A swollen lip

8 They're no swots and one of the band has admitted he left school without a single O level. Who is he?

Howard Donald ✓

9 Football crazy Mark tried out for two local teams as a lad. Which were they?

Manchester United & Rochdale ✓

10 Mark's mum told him to give up his struggling pop career to become what?

a) A deep sea diver
(b) A bank clerk
c) A dustman

11 How many people turned up to see the band's first show in Huddersfield?

a) 200
(b) 20
c) 2,000

12 How does manager Nigel keep the guys from getting big-headed?

a) By making them sing nursery rhymes
b) By taking fans home to dinner
c) By making them do the washing-up ✓

13 Their first single, 'Do What U Like', didn't even reach the Top Eighty. How far did it get?

82 ✓

14 Which pint-sized Aussie pop singer does Jason Orange have a crush on?

Kylie Minogue ✓

15 What was the name of the band Gary and Mark formed before Take That?

The Cutest Rush ✓

16 Which member of the band has a sister called Tracy?

Mark Owen ✓

17 Whose father was a Latin American dance teacher?

Howard Donald ✓

18 He's got two spaniels and he's hooked on chocolate and Chinese food. Who is he?

Gary Barlow ✓

19 Three of the band members still live at home. Who?

Howard, mark and Robbie ✓

20 Jason has a twin brother. Who is older and by how much? twenty minutes ✓

21 Which now sadly defunct magazine did the band appear nearly nude in?

Number 1 ✓

22 What is Robbie's middle name?

Peter ✓

23 What were the guys smeared with during the video for 'Do What U Like'?

Jelly ✓

24 Which member of the band is keen on rollerblading?

Robbie Williams ✓

25 The guys were smuggled past thousands of fans out of the HMV store in Manchester. What were they wearing as disguise?

(a) Police uniforms
b) Gorilla suits
c) Raincoats ✓

26 Which member of Take That loves girls with long dark hair, 'like Yasmin le Bon'?

Jason orange ✓

27 How many songs are there on *Take That and Party*?

Thirteen ✓

28 Which member of the band has a pet lizard called Nirvana?

Mark Owen ✓

29 When did the band first sign their contract with
Nigel Martin-Smith?

September 1990 ✓

30 Whose mum suffered so badly after one of Take
That's concerts that she had to take pills for
inflammation of her eardrums?

Howard's mother ✓

31 Take That had only one single in the Top Ten before
'I Found Heaven'. What was it?

It only takes a minute ✓

32 Which seventies band did the original version of 'It
Only Takes a Minute'?

Tavares ✓

33 Which Take That member claims he went through
girlfriends like hot dinners at school, and has never
been in love? *Robbie Williams* ✓

34 Which craze in jeans fashion did Take That bring
back into style? *Turn-ups* ✓

35 Take That turned his classic melody 'Could It Be
Magic' into an up-tempo hit. Name the middle-aged
singer/song-writer.

Barry Manilow ✓

36 He is going to return the compliment with his own
version of which Take That ballad?

A million love songs ✓

37 Jason and Howard break-danced together in
another group before Take That. What was it called?

a) Boneshaker
b) Street Heat
c) Street Beat

38 Two members of the band don't come from
Manchester. Who are they and where do they come
from? Gary (Chesire) and Robbie
(Stroke on Trent)

39 What is Jason's favourite motto?

a) Too many cooks spoil the broth.
b) Variety is the spice of life.
c) Don't kill the goose that laid the golden
   egg.

40 Which rock legend did Mark impersonate as a
youngster? Elvis Presley

41 Which Take That song features the lyrics 'I found
love with somebody else's girl'?

I've found heaven

42 What is Robbie's favourite soap?

a) Coronation Street
b) Emmerdale
c) Eldorado

43 Which member of the band had hypnosis to beat his fear of cars?

Gary Barlow ✓

44 Which member of the band has a dolphin tattoo?

Mark owen ✓

45 How many other youngsters were competing against Robbie to win a place in Take That?

a) 20
b) 200
c) 2,000 ✓

$\frac{45}{45}$

ANSWERS TO QUIZ

1 c

2 Gary

3 Two years

4 Howard

5 *Come Dancing*

6 Robbie

7 a

8 Howard

9 Manchester United and Rochdale

10 b

11 b

12 c

13 Eighty-two

14 Kylie Minogue

15 The Cutest Rush

16 Mark

17 Howard

18 Gary

19 Howard, Mark and Robbie

20 Jason, by twenty minutes

21 *No. 1*

22 Peter

23 Jelly and ice cream

24 Robbie

25 a

26 Jason

27 Thirteen

28 Mark

29 September 1990

30 Howard's mum

31 'It Only Takes a Minute'

32 Tavares

33 Robbie

34 Turn-ups

35	Barry Manilow	39	b
36	'A Million Love Songs'	40	Elvis Presley
		41	'I Found Heaven'
37	c	42	a
38	Gary (Frodsham, Cheshire) and Robbie (Stoke-on-Trent)	43	Gary
		44	Mark
		45	c

HOW DID YOU SCORE?

40 or more

Consider yourself a true
super-fan!

20—39

You're obviously a loyal
fan, and well on your way
to total dedication.

5—19

Could do better — some
extra Take That homework
might be in order.

Under 5

Call yourself a fan? Are you
sure we're talking about
the same band?

ACKNOWLEDGEMENTS

Many people helped in getting this book together. Among those I would particularly like to single out is Louise Johncox, my researcher, who made an intrepid and invaluable contribution to the book. Other thanks go to Don Short, my agent, and Val Hudson and Karen Whitlock at HarperCollins.

Thanks must also go to all the members of Take That, Gary Barlow, Mark Owen, Robbie Williams, Jason Orange and Howard Donald, who gave me such great interviews, as well as their manager Nigel Martin-Smith and PR Loretta de Souza. Other people who were helpful include Pete Waterman, Ro Newton and Carolyn Norman.

Hundreds of newspaper and magazine articles were used as secondary sources to my own interviews, including the *Daily Mirror*, *Smash Hits*, *Just Seventeen*, *Big*, *TV Hits*, *Sunday Magazine*, the *Daily Star*, the *Sun*, the *Daily Mail* and the *Daily Express*.

The Take That Fact File

The author and the publishers would like to thank the following photographers and picture agencies for allowing us to reproduce their photographs:

Xavier Pictures Ltd
Retna Pictures
All Action
London Features International Ltd
Famous
Claude Gassian (Paris)
Benoît Staes (Brussels)